The Heliotrope: or, Pilgrim in pursuit of health. Cantos first and Second. (Hymn to the Virgin. Lines to a Sicilian air. Charybdis.) [By William Beattie.]

William Beattie, William M.D. Beattie

The Heliotrope: or, Pilgrim in pursuit of health. Cantos first and Second. (Hymn to the Virgin. Lines to a Sicilian air. Charybdis.) [By William Beattie.]

Beattie, William
British Library, Historical Print Editions
British Library
Beattie, William M.D.
1833
80 p. ; 12°.
994.k.47.

The BiblioLife Network

GUIDE TO FOLD-OUTS, MAPS and OVERSIZED IMAGES

THE

HELIOTROPE;

OR,

PILGRIM IN PURSUIT OF HEALTH.

" Here," said the Physician, " art can do little—climate may do
much. Let him pass the seas, loiter a while on the Mediterranean, and,
after some months' cautious experience, fix on some retreat—Tuscan
or Sicilian. In a word, let him imitate the HELIOTROPE—*keep his face
constantly towards the sun;* and the SUN—always a warm friend—
may prove the best PHYSICIAN !"

CANTOS FIRST AND SECOND.

LIGURIA—HETRURIA—CAMPANIA—CALABRIA.

LONDON:

PRINTED FOR

LONGMAN, REES, ORME, BROWN, GREEN, AND LONGMAN,

PATERNOSTER ROW.

1833.

O dulce divûm munus, O SALUS Hebes
Germana! Tuque PHŒBE morborum terror
Pythone cæso, sive tu magis Pæan
Libenter audis, hic tuus sacerdos est.

Whiting, Beaufort House, Strand.

TO ASPASIA.

Pommi con fama oscura, o con illustre:
Sarò qual fui: vivrò com' io son visso . . .

What is *life?*—like a flower, with the bane in its bosom,

To-day full of promise—to-morrow it dies!—

And *health*—like the dew-drop that hung on its blossom,

Survives but a night, and exhales to the skies!—

How oft 'neath the bud, that is brightest and fairest,

The seeds of the canker in embryo lurk!

How oft at the root of the flower that is rarest—

Secure in its ambush—the worm is at work!——

The harvest is sown—but the hand of the sower

   Lies cold on the glebe that should gather the sheaf!

And levelled, like grass 'neath the steel of the mower,

   Man sinks to the earth with his joy and his grief.

Yet firm be my bearing!—superior to sorrow—

   Let the bright star of promise illumine my way!

And the watchword of life be—The joys of to-morrow

   Shall richly compensate the cares of to-day!

Hope beckons to climes where the flowers never wither—

   Where the Sun hath his temples—Hygeïa her shrine:

But the heart and the minstrel depart not together—

   The Pilgrim may roam—but the spirit is *thine!*

And the farther I wander, the fonder I cherish

   Each thought that reminds me of *thee*, and the past!

Thy love—though the visions of fancy may perish—

   Shall cheer my horizon and shine to the last!—

CANTO FIRST.

———

The Poem, of which the following Cantos are offered as a specimen, is an attempt to trace the progress of a traveller in pursuit of Health; to delineate his moral complexion and temperament; and to depict the various scenes and associations presented to him in the course of his peregrinations.

The work was composed among the localities it commemorates, and with no higher aim than to divert the mind of the writer from severer studies, and to preserve a faithful record of impressions resulting from change of climate. The Author is fully aware that, as a stranger in the field of literature, he must owe to the courtesy and indulgence of the reader what he cannot claim for his poetical merit; but hopes, that if, on perusal, little be found to conciliate praise, little will be found to provoke censure.

Should the reception of the portion now submitted to public suffrage, justify a presumption that more would be acceptable; the remaining Cantos of the Poem, wherein the Pilgrim enters on a less frequented track, will shortly follow.

———

ARGUMENT.

CANTO FIRST.

SPRING scenes and impressions in England — The contrast—
The subject introduced—His character—Cultivated mind—Ardent
imagination—Inordinate love of study—The consequences thereby
induced — Consumption, its first symptoms — The Pilgrim quits
England—Embarks for Italy—Night at sea—His progress—Apostrophe to the Ocean—The Bay of Biscay—A hurricane—The ship
in danger—Loss of life—Morning—The storm abates—Signals of distress—The contrast—Marine animals at sunset—The shark—Shores
of the Mediterranean—Evening impressions—Alps—Monaco—The
breeze from land—St. Remo's bell—The pilot's hymn—Italian skies—
Morning—First view of Genoa—Its progressive developement—First
appearance—Strong impressions—The ship anchors in the bay—
Sketch of the surrounding scenery—The Pilgrim disembarks—Vesper
service in the cathedral—Sketch—Genoa—Retrospective sketch—Her
rise—Progress—Decline—Present state—Prospects—Contrasts and
reflections—ANDREA DORIA—Sunset on the Apennines—The bay—
Scenes and reflections at midnight—Night—The hermit—Dawn—
Morning scenes—Columbus's dream—Village shrine—Relics—Votive
offerings—Capuchin friar—Portrait—The galley slave—Genoa in the
distance—Tuscan frontier—Hetruria—Characteristics of—Apostrophe
to—Its hold upon the imagination—Sovereigns and learned men—
Santa Croce — Florence — Galileo — Danté—Alfieri—Milton—Rural
Pictures—The vale of Arno—The sun and sky—Pisa—DUOMO—
Leaning tower—CAMPO-SANTO—The resort of invalids—Apostrophe
to—Sketch of a Tuscan villa—Conclusion.

ERRATUM.

Stanza LXIX., p. 37, line 8., for " *wears*" read " *wear*."

THE

HELIOTROPE.

CANTO FIRST.

Nescia mens hominum fati sortisque futuræ !—Æn. x.

O ego quantus eram, gelidi cum stratus ad ARNI
Murmura, populeumque nemus, qua mollior herba,
Carpere nunc violas, nunc summas carpere myrtos.—MILTON.

I.

'TIS NATURE's jubilee—the voice of Spring
  New robes creation: through the forest flushing
Flowers shed their perfume—birds on joyful wing
  Gladden the grove: while streams, like music gushing,
Their crystal currents o'er the valley fling.—
  Flocks bleat around;—to verdant pastures rushing,
Herds quit the stall—the hind his winter hearth—
And Hope's exulting spirit walks the earth !

B

II.

Forth fares the wild bee—wakes the mingled sound
     Of busy life abroad : each budding bough
Drops melody : with golden ringlets crowned
     Sweet waves the acacia !—Lover's whispered vow
And jest, and jocund lay are breathed around.—
     O'er the blue sea, and on the mountain's brow,
Skims the light bark—and bounds the trooping deer—
And stately floats the wild swan on the meer!

III.

The violet, hyacinth, and primrose pale
     Garland each hedgerow ;—crimson on the hill
Glows the rich almond blossom : o'er the vale
     The skies drop fatness—buds their sweets distil :
And hark ! at eve, the fresh-tuned nightingale
     Prolongs her wakeful note—till, on the rill
And ruddy lake bright imaged—the warm morn
Has scared the plaintive minstrel from her thorn.

IV.

But Spring—while thus it clothes the fields with bloom —

And crowns the tree with clustered buds—bestows

Nor life, nor genial warmth, where hand of doom

Sits heavy on the heart, which—like the rose

Untimely blanched of all its sweet perfume—

No vernal voice of inspiration knows !

And such was *he*—the stricken of his race—

Whose pilgrim steps the muse would here retrace.

V.

Science and Song had smiled upon his vows,

High aspirations fanned the generous flame :

And, in the cause enlightened minds espouse,

He followed in his fathers' steps to fame—

But followed in that arduous path which ploughs

Untimely furrows—to achieve a name !

The stream of lore with thirsty lip he quaffed—

Drank at its fount, but poison with the draught !

VI.

Each circling moon evolved fresh germs of taste:

But—with the culture planted—wasting care,

And midnight oil, and mental vigils, traced

Prophetic lines upon his forehead fair!—

Yet deemed he not Ambition is life's waste—

Nor Learning's trophies pageants of despair;

Whose subtle flame—though drawn from source divine—

Even while it sanctifies, consumes the shrine.

VII.

Still undismayed, he nursed the hallowed fire,

And swept with steadier hand the magic key;

Beauty inspired, and taste refined his lyre—

Till passion overflowed in poesy!

While, hovering round him, Fancy's airy choir—

Through dazzling dreams of immortality—

Shed their prospective glory on his sight,

Till long their votary's lamp outlived the night!

VIII.

Still with his fevered pulse, fresh hopes kept pace—
    'Mid fears confessed, and tears in secret streaming—
And dark thoughts saddening every kindred face,
    His with the buoyancy of hope was beaming !—
Lands of renown—the Muses' dwelling-place—
    Like gorgeous visions on his soul were gleaming—
Whose godlike records, deeds, and lore sublime
Arose like landmarks in the sea of time !—

IX.

And flashed the while, upon his ardent gaze
    Lights intellectual—mystic forms that haunted
His day-dreams, circled with immortal bays !
    And more he gazed—the more his spirit panted
With sacred fervour kindled by the lays
    Of lips inspired—implored a boon which, granted
Brings sorrow with its sunshine—and the moon
Of melancholy skies for promised noon !
                    *   *   *

X.

Such might not last.   Worn with intensity
   Of lengthened study—him the vernal ray
Revived not, that revived the forest tree;
   Nor health restored the summer's ripened day.—
Compassed with cares, from which he longed to flee,
   And ills that gathered strength from each delay,
Yet still he lingered—round him quaintly piled,
Hope reared her structures—wayward fancies smiled.

XI.

What though his mind transmitted in his lay
   Outlive the minstrel ?—From his genial spring,
The mildew's taint no song could chase away,
   Nor from his bosom pluck the canker's sting !
The fruits of thought are premature decay.—
   And now where fairest hopes were blossoming
The blight is fallen :—the hectic's fitful streak
With flush portentous lightens o'er his cheek.

*   *   *

XII.

But still he paused: for they who ministered
   In healing office, held his hopes elate:
While some—unskilled in Coan lore—averred
   With every watch they saw advancing fate!
And now they talked of change, but still deferred,
   Advised, consulted, and resolved—*to wait!*
And, thus, how oft the sick man's couch around,
Delays augment the medicable wound!

XIII.

The Spring has passed—the Summer leaf is sear—
   Autumn's pale livery drapes the forest tree:
Stern Winter comes with tempests in his rear—
   The stricken hath but one resource—to flee!
And follow, where, in balmy hemisphere,
   The summer lingers on Hetruria's sea—
Where brighter day revives the drooping form,
And vernal flowers outlive the winter storm.

XIV.

The face of friends—each fair and favoured spot

    By nameless ties endeared!—lake, vale, and river,

The waving forest, lawn, and silvan grot—

    Spoke with a voice that made it hard to sever!

And, each in turn surveyed, the question smote

    Keen on his startled ear—" Part we for ever ?" . . .

His heart betrayed a momentary qualm,

But checked the struggle—and regained its calm !

XV.

Not his the soul that reckless could resign

    Yon cliffs—upreared like bulwarks for the free !

But as they sank into their subject brine

    The tear sprang tributary to his e'e :—

" The land of Liberty and Virtue's shrine

    Shall ne'er upbraid apostacy in me !—

Where'er my pilgrim steps may rest or roam,—

Forget me, Heaven, if I forget my home !

XVI.

" Strong are the foes that I must grapple with—

  Whom I, perchance, but flee to be o'ertaken

More feeble by my flight !   Yet, in the pith

  Of my life's tree, if spring hath ceased to waken

The wonted sap—why tempt the stormy frith?—

  Why hoist a sail so many winds have shaken ?

This have I learnt: The heart that hope deceives

All dangers sooth—and every change relieves !"

XVII.

And now unmoored, the stately *Runnemede*

  Bounds blithly on with her exulting crew :

Ocean expands, the glimmering shores recede—

  Till the last landmarks vanish from his view,

But, lingering long in fancied shadows, feed

  Fond themes to nature and affection true !—

That mingled light, and loneliness, impart,

Which sooth the memory while they melt the heart.

XVIII.

Light and the land are gone: Night's galaxy,

    Gorgeous with spangled stars, aloft is blazing:

The freshening breeze, with its rude minstrelsy,

    Sings shrilly 'mid the shrouds; the billow raising

Its hoarse response, explodes in boisterous glee !—

    The helmsman, o'er the dim horizon gazing,

Invokes propitious winds :—and, crowding sail,

The gallant ship rides on before the gale.—

XIX.

Pleasure nor profit were it here, to tell

    How passed his nights and days—suffice they passed.

Still onward, like a moving citadel,

    Obsequious winds impelled the winged mast;

And strange the Pilgrim's joy, when the full swell

    Of blustering waves sang chorus to the blast !—

To him, their harmony seemed more divine

Than ever soared from consecrated shrine !

XX.

Mysterious Ocean ! ever changeful main !
    Boundless and vast, and, like eternity,
Hoarding within thy dark unfathomed reign
    Wonders deep veiled from mortal scrutiny !—
Thunder, and storm, and lightning in thy train,
    Destruction and creation wait on thee !
Here, thou dost gulf the green and stable earth,
There, givest in sport its phantom islands birth !—

XXI.

Twelve days at sea—dark signs in sky and ocean
    Announced impending dangers to our crew :
Slow marshalled on the horizon, clouds in motion
    Gathered—condensed—and into blackness grew—
Then burst the bellowing thunder's dread explosion,
    And heaven's blue concave—blotted from the view—
Brooded in night—above no star was sparkling ;
Around—below—the sea frowned wild and darkling.

XXII.

Anon the whirlwind rushed !—the billows under

   Shivered in fragments tossed their foam on high—

Deep—'mid the tortured waters torn asunder—

   The gulf yawned horrible !—while, from the sky

Fierce lightnings flashed and the hoarse growling thunder

   Swept through the welkin in wild revelry—

Bursting responsive, as the burning leven

Scattered its arrowy shafts athwart the heaven !—

XXIII.

Day passed—and midnight came:—and downward gushing

   The sky unsluiced its torrents: flash on flash

The lightnings gleamed—with their fierce pinion brushing

   The groaning shrouds: when hark! with startling crash—

'Mid howling winds and roaring billows crushing

   Man's smothered voice—invading breakers dash

Our bulwarks from the board :—the pinnace stove—

And canvass rent—the vessel recled, and *drove!*

XXIV.

But proudly vaulting through the mountain surge
    Her British oak defies the ruffian blast,
While prompt obedience—skill—and courage urge
    The drifting keel, and man the giddy mast.—
The helm has answered !—from the *breaker*'s verge
    She rights !—she flies ! The deathful hour is past !
But still the storm that strews the bay with wreck,
Baffles our strength, and sweeps the groaning deck !

XXV.

' It comes !—quick to your post !"—De Courcy spoke—
    Swift as the word, each hardy seaman sprung
Elastic to his task.—The tempest broke
    Right o'er our bows—the eddying vessel swung,
Ridged on a foaming precipice !—The shock
    Of desperate waters, on our quarter flung,
Shook every beam !—the stript and straining pine
Bent like an osier in the sweeping brine !

XXVI.

But where was he—our helm's bold mariner ?—

 Gulfed in the surge—his dread and sudden grave !

With strong, but hopeless struggle, on our ear

 His death-cry wildly struck—till the hoarse wave

Hushed him for ever in his boisterous bier !—

 Spurning each feeble hand that strove to save

Our sinking comrade—the remorseless sea

Answered our sorrow with wild mockery ! . . . .

XXVII.

The storm has howled his requiem—ne'er again

 To guide the helm, nor brave the tempest's frown !

Nor gather laurels on the billow's mane !—

 Yet he sleeps well ! . . . Now, slowly, softening down,

The wind respires in gusts—the hurricane

 Foldeth its wings—reluctantly to crown

Our growing hopes ! But still the mountain swell

Tosses our bark 'twixt gulf and pinnacle !

XXVIII.

At length, from Ortegal's bluff headlands wheeling, 1
   Day's kindling car rose slowly on the view;
And, like a flood, o'er Alps and ocean stealing
   The welcome morn her gorgeous mantle threw—
To man's rapt eye that Majesty revealing
   At whose behest the howling storm withdrew !
And like creation's dawn, from chaos springing,—
Life, beauty, harmony, and order bringing !—

XXIX.

Now, like a wild swan hastening on her way—
   Spreading her wings to meet the wind's caress,
Once more her course the stately vessel lay,
   Crowning the swell of ocean's wilderness.—
And oft, while clearing that tempestuous bay,
   Some lingering signal of the night's distress
Smote on our heart, and drew our helm aside,—
But, to our friendly hail no voice replied !

XXX.

The scene how changed!. Where rending thunders ran,

   Now—like a child lulled on maternal breast—

With cheek unchafed by the fierce *Tramontan*,   2

   The billow sleeps; while o'er its glassy crest,

Yon scaly brood, led by leviathan,

   Pursue their gambols in the glowing west;

And, scattered from their scales, prismatic dies—

Brief coruscations—flash the evening skies!

XXXI. ·

And lo—stanch to his track and hard astern,

   Dogging the ship insatiate—the grim shark

Swims in our wake: fitful, we can discern

   His shifting—sly manœuvres round the bark!

While some with bullet—some with baited yarn ·

   Prepare his banquet!—From the bulwark—hark!—

A shot has told—and, weltering in his blood,

The struggling monster churns the boiling flood!—.

＊　＊　＊

XXXII.

Day sinks in roses :—on the Pilgrim glancing   3
   Rich and romantic landscapes glimmer near ;
In airy whirl, retiring or advancing,
   Above, the sea-bird's clamorous brood career—
Beyond, the barge on glassy waters dancing,
   And, from the heights, the distant muleteer
With bells, and barcarole, and measured oar,
Blend the night melodies of sea and shore !

XXXIII.

Beneath yon gaily peopled cliffs, the sea—
   Spread like a mighty mirror, where the snows
Of the proud Alps lie cradled tranquilly—
   Gathers the mountain streams beneath our bows ;
And there—for princely feats and sanctity
   Long famed—the clustered towers of Monaco's   4
Gray pyramid—a palace, fort, and shrine—
Fling their long shadows o'er the ruddy brine.—

c

XXXIV.

Ever, at vesper hour and morning prime,

   The mountain breeze comes freighted with perfume—

All redolent of that delicious clime

   Wherein the immortal aloe loves to bloom !   5

On every hill, the forts of olden time

   Transmuted to the fanes of modern Rome—

But half forgotten—like their priests or kings—

Proclaim the changeful stamp of earthly things !

XXXV.

Hark ! solemn notes upon the night-wind swelling,

   Salute the Pilgrim's ear—St. REMO's bell !   6

Of pious shrift, and sweet indulgence telling—

   And midnight mass, and orisons whose spell

The demon's wiles, and Ocean's fury quelling,

   Can snatch the shipwrecked from the brink of hell !

The pilot heard the sound, and crossed him thrice—

Then poured in tune his wonted sacrifice :—

1.

The mid-watch is set ;

O'er the dark heaving billow

Night's shadows have met—

Then awake from thy pillow !

Let the bell of St. Remo

Give warmth to thy zeal—

At the voice of thy patron

Kneel, mariner, kneel !

2.

From his shrine on the cliff,

In thy joyance or cumber,

He pilots thy skiff—

Though its master may slumber !—

When—like weeds o'er the waters—

Storm-drifted we reel,

The dark cloud he scatters—

Kneel, mariner, kneel !

c 2

3.

Though the mast like an osier

Be stript in the gale—

One sign from his crosier

Can rescue thy sail!

Then, to holy St. Remo,

Who wakes for thy weal,

And lays the loud tempest!

Kneel, mariner, kneel!

4.

From the welkin and wave,

As we bow to his relic—

From the mountain and cave,

Hark! voices angelic!

" In doubt, and in danger,

To guard and to cheer—

Thy Star, 'mid the darkness,

St. Remo is near!"—

XXXVI.

How calm the night!—clothed in its loveliest hue,
　Spangled with stars, and liquidly serene!
Such as enraptured GALILEO's view,
　Fresh worlds unfolding!—Ever as the scene
Exchanged with morn, the charm was ever new,
　For now the vessel ploughed the blue TYRRHENE
And, when the sun glanced from Liguria's sky,
Twas scene, I wot, to charm the saddest eye!

XXXVII.

At first a faint cloud on the horizon's rim;
　Then, slowly mounting from the Ocean's marge,
Ramparts, and towers, and temples glimmered dim,
　And forts that told of many a hostile charge!—
The Mole—the Bay!—and there, in gala trim,
　Felucca, gondola, and gilded barge—
A festal fleet!—Beyond, in purple light,
Proud GENOA soars—a glad and gorgeous sight!　7

XXXVIII.

And nearer, as with joyous oar we drew,

　　The whispered welcome met us on our way—

Around us balmy odours Zephyr blew

　　From honied hills, where hives make holiday!

But, lovelier yet the varied landscape grew,

　　As evening shadows spanned the glassy Bay,

And the bewildered vision wandered o'er

The clustered charms of that romantic shore!

XXXIX.

The yards are manned—the flapping canvass furled;

　　The slackening prow scarce frets the wave to foam:

Before me—gleaming like a fairy world—

　　Bright with each charm that woos the heart to roam;

With treasured art, and Nature's wealth impearled—

　　The poet, painter, patriot's genial home!

ITALIA! gazing thus on thine and thee,

How mounts the blood with spring-tide buoyancy!

XL.

Entranced upon the galiot's silent bow,

 Long gazed the pilgrim with delighted eye ;

Where spire and tower their fair proportions throw,

 Traced on the blue of that ethereal sky,

Whose pillars—yonder pyramids of snow,

 The trackless regions of eternity—

Stand forth, gigantic guardians of a soil

Rich in the triumphs of man's noblest toil !—

* * *

XLI.

It is the hour when song and sunset meet—

 When stars are kindling, and the vesper chime

Gathers the worshipper from every street

 To crown, with hallowing rites, the ebb of Time !

And now, with panting heart, the Pilgrim's feet

 Have pressed the soil of that delicious clime—

Long pictured as the bright and promised land,

Where Health stood beckoning him with gifts in hand !—

XLII.

It is the hour when Beauty to the shrine

    Brings her oblation !—Hark, the swelling hymn !

The choral chant from the long pilgrim line—

    Each busy with his beads !—austere and grim,

Here plies the monk his ghostly discipline,

    Where dark eyes—such as snared the Seraphim—

And veil flung white from her hair's glossy coil,

Announce the Circè of Liguria's soil !—   8

XLIII.

Where'er the worship—lo, luxurious shrines—

    Gaudy with all that lavished gold may give !

Gemmed altars—sculptured walls, where the warm lines

    Of holy, or heroic patriots live !

While yon *Madonna*'s every trait combines   9

    The last perfection genius could achieve !

Well may the devotee believe—who kneels

Prone at her feet—she hears, and sees, and feels !—

XLIV.

Civic, and sacred pomp, where'er ye turn—

Science, and art, and power, and opulence—

All have their monuments—or domes that burn   10

In molten gold like NERO's !—all dispense

Most novel lustre—even the storied urn—

Disguising Death by its magnificence !

Proclaims its mortal record, traced in gems

Plucked from the brows of eastern diadems !—

XLV.

Matured by hardy virtues through long years,

LIGURIA's commerce stemmed the subject wave :

Her navy rode in triumph ; feuds and fears

Merged in one common cause : sage counsels gave

Her state its solid grandeur—such as rears

A race of patriots : while her wise and brave

Conspired for her adornment, till she shone

The dread of distant shores—the glory of her own

XLVI.

Arts rose, and Science ripened to rich fruit;

 And wealth, by patient industry amassed,

Was nobly lavished: Charity took root,   11

 And, kindred with her heavenly creed, halls vast

Endowed, and hallowed—to the poor man's suit

 Gave bread, and shelter from the world's cold blast:—

Honoured all worth—befriended all distress—

Cherished the widow—reared the fatherless!

XLVII.

Kings were her tributaries; every sea

 Unlocked its spoils to waft them to her breast:

The Doria led her fleet; and Freedom's tree,

 And freemen flourished, on her mountain crest

Intrenched impregnable: Prosperity

 Poured in her golden tide from east and west!—

Alas, how changed!—her deeds of other years

Are now a tale—a tale for woman's tears!—

XLVIII.

And here in secret, bitter tears are shed,

   Fresh, fruitless yearnings—weak resolves—again

To perish like a vapour !—O'er her head

   The brandished rod, and on her limbs the chain,

And in her heart distrust—despondence fed—

   She drags the wheel, that might have held the rein ;

And still might rule—united did she know

Her native strength, and dared to strike the blow !

XLIX.

Widowed and sad, the slave is in her gate—

   The stranger on her throne ;—the shackled limb

Clanks in her streets !—That once redoubted State

   Dreams in her dotage : void on Ocean's brim,

The DORIA's sculptured halls are desolate !   12

   Damp Freedom's hearth—hushed the triumphal hymn !

The glory he bequeathed—the blood he shed

Rouse not the living—can they wake the dead ?—

L.

Her golden sun is set : an age of brass—

    But forged in chains—succeeds her glorious day !

To rival marts the freighted galiots pass :

    The haughty merchant halts not in her bay—

That beauteous bay !—where once, upon its glass

    The keels of every shore reflected lay !—

But now her Moles in crumbling masses rise,

To tell how Commerce droops, where Freedom dies !

LI.

But hark, the watchword—LIBERTY, like morn,

    Though dimmed by passing shadows, dieth not !—

Again the elastic spirit, in its scorn

    Starting to life, shall raze the withering blot

That clouds her record, and exalt her horn

    Of slumbering strength !—The palace and the cot

Revive the songs of yore !—again the fire

Flashes indignant from Liguria's lyre !—

LII.

What eye has seen thee,—" City of Delight ?"   13

   Thy streets of palaces and seats of power;

Thy fort, or fane surmounting every height—

   Thy sunny slopes—thy beauty's ample dower !

Nor sadly turned aside to mark the night

   Gathering so fast on thy meridian hour—

The rank grass wave, and night's unhallowed herb

Mantling the courts of " Genoa the Superb !"

LIII.

But such the stamp and sport of destiny !—

   Power hath its dawn, and zenith, and decay:

Earth has no more : the forest's stateliest tree

   Sheds but its numbered leaves, then wastes away !

The loftiest mound of man's prosperity—

   The tombs of Egypt, piled on Pharaoh's clay—

Back to the earth, by Heaven's dread law impelled,

Behold them crumbling like the dust they held !—

LIV.

But here we pause:—and, Nature for our theme,

    Let sweeter meditations soothe the breast!

Unchanging, save in charms, she—when a dream—

    And but a dream is left us to attest

Man's faded glory—peoples wood and stream,

    And Heaven profound, and Earth's enamelled vest

With beauties—all so soothingly unfolded,

The pulse beats calm, to holy musings moulded!

LV.

Lingering in smiles, upon the Alpine snow,   14

    A rosy flood survives the parent day:

Like molten gold the Ocean gleams below!

    Then, in the deepening opal dies away!

There, lightly skimmed by many a rippling prow,

    The wave makes melody, and all the bay

Sparkles with stars; while Nature's voice in power

Inspires emotions sacred to the hour!—

LVI.

The scene invites—launch forth upon the tide
    While night surrounds thee in her starry noon!
But launch alone—and leave thy bark to glide,
    As lists the wave, along the bright lagoon;
Where, mirrored on its bosom like a bride,
    Fair Genoa gleams, and yon meridian moon
Rivals the day:—to thee, that hour shall teach
Truths unimbodied in terrestrial speech!—

LVII.

Far up the Apennine the forest heaves—
    Fanned by the breath, and flickering in the beam
Of starry skies—a wilderness of leaves!
    Through which, at intervals, the wayward stream
Leaps forth in silver!—O'er the city's eaves
    Sleep spreads her mantle: gyveless in his dream
The slave is free—stretched on the galley's bows,
Nor stripe, nor chain disturb his deep repose!

LVIII.

Congenial Night! beneath thy placid reign

   What trembling thoughts be breathed, what sorrows told?

Sealed lips that dare not to the sun complain

   In thy lone ear the secret heart unfold !—

To him who wears the crown or bears the chain—

   Sovereign or slave—thy glittering pall unrolled

Brings equal boon, so it doth bring—the best

Of all Heaven's gifts to mortal longings—*rest !*

LIX.

A secret voice pervades thee, lonely Night !—

   A language starry heavens alone impart ;

Inspiring lips of holy anchorite,

   And pouring balm on silent wounds that smart !

Oh ! when oppressed with sorrows exquisite,

   How tranquillizing thou to the lone heart !

How welcome to the wakeful, wounded sense

That owns no soother like thy eloquence !

*   *   *

LX.

From yon lone shrine, perched on the silent hill,   15
   Glimmers the hermit's votive lamp; and gushing
From orange grove, the nightingale's long trill
   Outlives the night!   The fountain's fitful rushing—
Morn's breath, and Ocean's drowsy murmurs fill
   Each pause between; till dawn in crimson blushing
Night's watch-fires fade; and Day, with warm embrace,
Uplifts the veil from Nature's radiant face!

LXI.

And now Liguria's shore, Liguria's sea—
   How beauteous both!   This, like an opal zone—
Where streamed of yore the standard of the free!
   That, once the proud emporium and the throne
Of all-connecting Commerce!—But the tree
   That bore her flag and fame to shores unknown,
Hath cruised its last!   Resigned its stately charge,
Weather and worms consume the SENATE's barge!
      * * *
D

LXII.

Here first, a schoolboy, o'er the waters blue,   16

   His future slave—the world's great Mariner,

Prophetic pastime, launched his frail canoe!—

   To wondering shores the future messenger!

Climes unimagined, constellations new,

   On Earth new boundaries destined to confer!

Yet reap at last from all the realms he gave

Scarce one neglected spot to yield a grave!

LXIII.

Here, while the stripling braced his mimic sail,

   Flashed on his mind, in its young energy,

His ocean-perils?—struggles with the gale?—

   Or deadlier struggles with man's treachery?

Dreamed he of myriad voices that should hail

   His thunders—heralding the Deity?

And greet the champion of that bold emprise,

With solemn rites and symbolled sacrifice?—

LXIV.

Even so 'tis told :— gray patriarchs believe

    The tale—that, haunted by a nameless spell,

Before the boy strange visions wont to weave

    Their web of mystery !—indescribable

In clime and hue—seas that appeared to heave

    With a new birth of worlds—where seemed to dwell

A race distinct, unknown, whose sunbright realm

Should burst like heaven on his adventurous helm !

LXXV.

Thus, haunted by the vision, and impelled

    By the strong spirit of emprise—'mid gleams

Of fitful fancies, in his grasp he held

    Regions that realized his wildest dreams,—

Widening Creation's bounds !—where rivers swelled,

    And green savannahs basked in golden beams—

Then went :—to friendly stars his sail unfurled,

And solved the mysteries of a second world !

LXVI.

'Tis morn!—and frequent from their olive bowers—
    Perched on some promontory o'er the tide—
White temples lift their patriarchial towers,   17
    The pilot's landmark and the pilgrim's guide !
And each endowed with some miraculous powers—
    Specific gifts—by gold thrice sanctified !
Where Penitence may wash her sins, and, shriven,
On steadier pinion shape her course to heaven.

LXVII.

Lo, crown, heart, crucifix, and costly braid,
    Rose-knots, and beads by holy Palmer strung
In Calvary's sepulchre—or hallowed shade
    Of rich Loretto—on its altar hung—
The votive pledge of swain and village maid !
    Tablets that may interpret for the tongue
Hopes fondly cherished !—dreams to memory dear—
Known but to heaven and their confessor's ear !

LXVIII.

There, solemn Capuchin, with cowl and cord,   18
    And wary eye, eludes the tempter's mesh:
By rigid fast, before his *reliques'* horde,
    Sorely he mortifies the stubborn flesh !
In vain for him rich viands press the board—
    In vain for him the grape is gushing fresh !
Too well he knows what banquet joys beget—
Where wine abounds—sly Satan throws his net.

LXIX.

The cell that shelters wearied age, does well :
    Not so, when manhood in a living tomb
Stifles those energies that else might swell
    The tide of freedom, and reverse the doom
That hangs upon his country—like a spell
    Blighting her hopes and withering all her bloom—
When youth, inglorious, mope the monkish task,
And wears the cowl whose fathers wore the casque !

LXX.

Is it thy squalid garb—thy tutored gait,

    Or mien sore mortified, that heaven requires?

Will forms or fasts, conciliate or create

    That paradise to which thy soul aspires?

No!—Born to work the welfare of the state—

    While thus the recreant from his post retires,

The patriot's heart in nobler purpose shrined,

Earns heaven, by earning blessings for his kind!

*   *   *

LXXI.

Bent 'neath his burden—bound on Ocean's brim

    To heave the blocking sand-bank from the wave,

And drag the clanking chain on his worn limb,

    Fettered and goaded creeps the galley-slave!   19

But heaviest in his slavery, presses him

    The thought, that chain must gall him to the grave!

Protracted life be still protracted pain,

And even repentance supplicate in vain!

LXXII.

Coupled in twain, the common doom they share,

   And singly wear the fetters forged by crime :

Yet notes the stranger in their haughty air

   Small sense of shame, or thought of better time !

A callous mirth, the growth of long despair—

   A recklessness, the spirit of their clime—

That dreads no doom, and nurtures no remorse,

Smothers reflection with a demon's force.

LXXIII.

Here, 'mid those desperate outlaws of the State—

   And once the terror of the mountains round—

Were two, in years unlike—but like in fate—

   Yet less by common doom than friendship bound :

Together, slavery lost its iron weight—

   Grief was forgotten, toil with patience crown'd :

The elder soothed, supported 'neath his load,

Him, who in manhood's steps scarce yet had trod.

LXXIV.

At length, what human clemency denied,
   Fate for the worn and withered heart achieved :
The younger drooped beneath his chain and died—
   The elder lived—to further pangs reprieved.—
He saw the body severed from his side
   With callous look—nor dropt a tear, nor grieved ;
Yet his limbs shook, and o'er his altered air,
Impetuous rushed the darkness of despair !

LXXV.

Wild frenzy seized his brain and knit his brow,—
   " Was it for this," he cried, " that years gone by
I've worn the felon's chain, nor shrunk till now ?
   'Mid all my pangs—that cell ne'er heard me sigh—
Yet—my stern soul subdued at last—I bow
   And falter in my fetters !   Liberty
Hath lost the sound that tempted to live on—
Since that which blunted life's keen shafts is gone !

LXXVI.

" Deeply I wronged his father—more than wronged—
　　For one base bribe, I sacrificed the son—
Saw him in shackles !—yet the more I longed
　　For other prey !—for I had sworn to run
The course of my revenge !—while conscience, thronged
　　With crimes, and harrowing dreams of horrors done,
Goaded me fiercely on !　Ye know the rest ;
I wore your chains—but, with unshackled breast !

LXXVII.

" Complaint I scorned—nor strove to mitigate
　　A doom my deeds had earned :—yet I had burst
Those baser bonds, and snatched me from my fate,—
　　Save that for him, the will to *be*, I nursed—
A longing, with my life commensurate—
　　That he might never know what hand had cursed
His earthly hopes !—and left its withering blot
Upon his name !—'Twas well, he knew me not.

LXXVIII.

" Once chained together,—pity touched my soul;

   I loved him—strange to say ! and strove to shed

O'er his dark night one ray of hope—my whole

   Heart strove to soothe—while it in secret bled !

We watched—toiled—wept together—shared the dole

   Man's mercy gave, and dignified as bread !

My task grew light :—methought the father smiled

Forgiveness—while I cheered his drooping child !

LXXIX.

" Hard as my heart hath been—'gainst pity steeled,

   Foe to my race—my own—and to the rood ;

Yet, have I—though on that small hope I build—

   Betwixt the victor and the victim stood !

Thrice freed the captive !—but, thus far annealed,

   I stop :—the rest were one long tale of blood !

I lived for him, who bore your chains for me,

But gone—my task is done—the slave is free !"

LXXX.

This said, a secret poniard from his sleeve,
　Saved from long scrutiny, and now unsheathed
Obedient to the word, leapt forth t'achieve
　The desperate resolve !　He struck—and breathed
Words choked with blood ! . . "'Tis thus that I retrieve
　My freedom—burst the gyves that long have wreathed
These limbs with sleepless agony !—that grave
Which tyrants dread—is shelter to the slave !"—
\#　\#　\#

LXXXI.

'Tis noon—thy last towers linger in my view,
　Liguria's capital !—And I must roam
Farther, though fainter ; the pursuit renew,
　Of what, much wooed, more hopeless hath become.
And I must bid thy sunbright shores adieu,
　As one that fain would rest, yet finds no home !
Still doomed to chase the phantom as it flies—
Still foster dreams no change can realize !

LXXXII.

But Hope, though distant still—is still before :
   While visions, kindled in her magic lens,
Their fair and fresh creations round me pour,
   And harmonize the fretful chords of sense.
Thus, following where she leads, I seek the shore
   Where harvest joys, reserved, shall recompense
Long travail :—Trust ! for patience still achieves
Its hallowed triumph for the heart that grieves.

LXXXIII.

Now, with steep toil, the Apennine is passed :
   And Spezzia's glassy gulf expands in view ;
Where, lingering for the long expected blast—
   And, sick of tranquil seas—the impatient crew
To welcome winds unfurl the sails at last,
   And lightly with the breeze their course pursue.
While in its speed beneath, the bounding prow
Meets the blue wave, and churns it into snow.

LXXXIV.

In yonder heights Carara's treasures lie;
　Massa's gray fortress crowns the feudal steep:
Sarzanna's ramparts fade; and on the eye
　Sweet vistas open o'er the Tuscan deep:
The peasant's rural home shines white on high;
　From rock to rock the mountain torrents leap:
While fruit and flower the self-same bough bestows,
And cultureless the grape's free nectar flows!

LXXXV.

Villas, and verdant meads, and hills of pine,
　Succeed to groves, that pour the treasured oil:—
Rapid and clear, brooks murmur to the brine,
　And on their banks, the peasant at his toil:
While pilgrim bands, beneath the clustering vine,
　Con marvellous creeds!—the produce of their soil;
While every hill that glimmers from afar
Mounts the tall cross, or hoists the flag of war.

LXXXVI.

And now my steps are on Hetruria's hills   20

   Of corn, and wine—whose harvests never fail—

And where the well requited peasant tills

   A grateful glebe, and breathes salubrious gale;

With frugal task each measured moment fills—

   Reclaims the waste—from the prolific vale,

Twice in his garner hoards the ripened sheaves,

And crowns his winter with unfading leaves!

LXXXVII.

And here, to me each hill is hallowed ground,

   Girt with a magic circle: Nature's dower,

And Man's immortal mind, have shed around

   Charms with the stamp of beauty, and the power

Of intellectual strength: here Arts have wound

   Their glory with the soil: with every bower

Immortal twined—familiar with each shade,

Here Taste and Genius hand in hand have strayed!

LXXXVIII.

Sweet Vale of Arno! of exalted mould
    What minds have sprung from thy maternal breast!
In counsel firm—in homebred virtue bold—
    In art supreme—in heavenly science blest!
Here Pallas her bright mysteries first unrolled,
    And dwelt a cherished and triumphant guest:
Here, fostering Science, while they ruled the helm,
Enlightened sovereigns swayed the Tuscan realm!

LXXXIX.

To thee, whose soil and city of the heart,
    Seem words of magic—raiseth every tongue
Its willing homage.—Thee, the painter's art
    Hath blazoned, and the poet's lay hath sung.
But who thy varied beauties shall impart!
    The land whose intellectual sky hath flung
Its light through earth! and to the bard and sage
Descended, like a glorious heritage!—

XC.

Sweet Vale of Arno! thou art all bestarred

    With names that rouse our inmost sympathy!

The banished DANTE, as a last reward,   21

    Longed but to take his last repose in thee,

Yet longed in vain!—Even our divinest Bard   22

    In his long night remembered Fiesolè!

While Florence with her classic Vale and Stream,

And Vallombrosa, lingered in his dream!

XCI.

Thy balmy summer, and the glittering throng

    That stud thy heavens, were banquet to his eyes—

Subject whereby to shape the immortal Song

    That pictured earth, while earth was paradise!

Here, while a pilgrim in thy shades, and strong

    In heaven's inspiring strength, bright phantasies

Of future glory on his spirit rose

That warmed his genius and consoled his woes!

*　*　*

XCII.

In Santa Croce's shrine the Pilgrim kneels—
　　There leaves the unshackled mind at will to range
Through distant vistas, where the past reveals
　　The eventful page !—the various lapse and change
Since of her bondage Freedom broke the seals !
　　And *mind* awakening—lore, and mysteries strange
Repaid her patriot sages :—here they lie—
The last bright stars of her proud galaxy !

XCIII.

Through yon dim arch, pours Evening's rosy gleam,
　　And GALILEO's bust refracts its course ;
Whereon it lingers with enamoured beam—
　　Gilding his urn, who scanned its secret source !
Who made the planets his impassioned theme,
　　And dared of starry worlds the dread discourse !
The dazzling tracks of ether trod alone—
Till the bright vision overwhelmed his own !—　　23

* * *

E

XCIV.

Hetrurian Tempé!   Who hath ever trod
 With soul uncharmed thy rich and classic bowers,
Brilliant as those that formed man's first abode,
 Ere sorrow darkened life's ambrosial hours!—
Here droops the vine beneath its purple load,
 Here Spring hath strewn a wilderness of flowers!
Here soil, and scene, and sunshine realize
All that her bards have feigned of Paradise!

XCV.

Here cheerful Industry has fixed her seat:
 Forest and field, their bounteous products pour:
What most delights the eye and ear to meet
 Gladdens the pilgrim!   Grouped at every door
Weaving the strawy web, or chanting sweet
 Some anthem Metastasio sang of yore,
Fair maidens welcome thee—and lay like theirs,
I rede thee, list—if thou hast many cares!

XCVI.

Here, from their hills when Morn's transparent veil
    Is softly gathered from the green champaign,
Her grateful voice the *contadini* hail
    And light, and welcome labour cheer the plain !
There on the stream they hoist the snowy sail—
    And here their daughters guide the household wain,
Whose cheeks eclipse Aurora's in their bloom—
Whose eyes outrival their dark beaver's plume.

XCVII.

Hither the spell-bound ALFIERI led,   24
    First of the powers of song enamoured grew :
Exchanged the palace for the peasant's shed—
    From pomp, to Nature's simple haunts withdrew :
Here life—love—language—all his passion fed
    For native melody;—here, 'mid the few
But favoured votaries of the Tuscan Muse,
He breathed new life, and drank inspiring dews.—

XCVIII.

Hail to thee, land of promise!—on my eyes

   Stretching 'twixt snowy Alps and sunny main!

Where morning breaks from ever clement skies,

   And brightly sets—as bright to rise again!

Where Beauty revels in her richest guise—

   And seasons in harmonious order reign:

Where, as her own rapt minstrels sing, the rose

Through winter tide, unwithered, buds and blows.—

XCIX.

Sun of the South! here, in thy native sky,

   Benignly bright! no lingering cloud is sailing

Yon deep, blue vault, to meet thy radiant eye!

   Here to man's gaze, thy glorious face unveiling,

Fresh hopes are fostered by the Zephyr's sigh:

   Here, the deep labyrinth of sense regaling,

Thy balmy breath and vivifying ray

Imbue the soul with renovated day!

C.

As bright on thy triumphant march thou glowest,

   As when the Etruscan fire flashed on thy shrine ;

Glorying in thy eternal youth, thou knowest

   Change, nor decay ! warmed in thy ray benign

Earth teems with life—perennial flowers thou sowest—

   And all that Summer banquets on is thine !

Thy beams imprint the flower and fire the gem,

And bind with glory Nature's diadem !—

CI.

Hither, from colder climes thy smile to share,   25

   Age, pining youth, and stricken beauty fly !

And, while their native sun sets in despair,

   Hail its revival in thy balmy sky.—

And lo, what faint and wasted forms are there,—

   Flitting like shadows in the pilgrim's eye !

And sheltering in her shade—their last retreat—

Great PISA's plain—Hygëia's favoured seat !

CII.

Beauty and health—life's brittle heritage—
  How quick ye pass! Here, by the wave reclined,
And lingering out her hopeless pilgrimage,
  Yet breathing fancied health with every wind—
Droops England's exiled rose! Though doomed to wage
  Unequal warfare—still her polished mind—
Mirror of every intellectual grace—
Reflects a settled sunshine on her face.

CIII.

She—like the almond-tree, all prematurely   26
  Bursting in flower, ere yet a sheltering leaf
Springs from the bough to bid it bloom securely
  And shield its blossom—beautiful and brief!
Ripened with fairest promise! Ah, how surely
  Our hearts reposed!—no sign foreboded grief!
The vernal rose upon her cheek she wore—
But with the canker folded in its core!

CIV.

Trust not the fresh, but meteor flush that plays
  Around the lip, and lights the languid eye!
It shines not as the pledge of happy days—
  But comes—the harbinger of danger nigh!
That hectic tint which on her cheek delays
  Is but the crimson on a vernal sky,
Which we—fond gazers on its rosy light—
Mistook for opening day!—and lo, 'tis night.

CV.

Thou, whom a breath can injure, or may bless—
  (Thus speaks the sage) on whom the summer's balm
Descends with healing strength—thy vows address,
  Where, in their crescent channel, clear and calm
Seaward the Arno's limpid waters press;
  There, shade and perfume from the vine and palm
Have woven a bower; and there the kindly beam
Invites repose, and cheers the pilgrim's dream.   27

CVI.

There, 'neath thy lattice, in the bright day sleeping,

    The river's breath shall cool thy fevered cheek;

And, when at night thy pensive vigils keeping,

    Its whisper, like a soothing voice shall speak.

But wisely shun yon bank, where, chilly sweeping,

    The *Tramontana* flies on pinions bleak!

And in the sun—thy sole and last resource—

Abide thy fate, and patient keep thy course!

CVII.

But hark! aloft from yon miraculous Tower,   28

    The chime that calls to prayer is just begun!

How dread o'er fated roofs its columns lower—

    Bent in obeisance to the setting sun!

As if to prostrate at the appointed hour

    Man and his works!   Yet still they pass, nor shun

The menaced path: while from its base, with awe

And fearful presage, stranger steps withdraw!

CVIII.

Struck with the sight, scaled with ambitious zeal—
　　The pilgrim lingers on its marble height,
Still vibrating with the loud vesper peal.
　　And ne'er have scenes more blooming blessed the sight
Than there on his enchanted vision steal—
　　All richly mellowed, as the waning light
Deepens each shadow, and with sapphire beam
Bronzes the grove, and gilds the Tuscan stream.

CIX.

Again, at matin hour the scene he sought,
　　While soared on high the choral voice of morn:
And long with curious eye and quickened thought
　　Surveyed the *Duomo*'s richly marbled bourn—
Its sculptured aisles by Grecian chisel wrought—
　　Its fretted vaults on Parian columns borne:
Then sought with slow and superstitious tread
The CAMPO-SANTO—city of the Dead!　　29

CX.

For much betimes, it profits to forsake

   The world's vain ways :—these cloisters have a tone—

A thrilling voice that makes the spirit quake

   In its clay tenement !—Here, sauntering on,

Such sad, but salutary thoughts awake

   As men from pulpit-lesson rarely con.—

Grieve I my dead ?—For dust do I repine?

Oh, here be thoughts to calm each grief of mine.

CXI.

And lo, what names in classic phrase enrolled !—

   What laboured epitaphs incrust that wall !—

All good, and great, and virtuous—and 'tis told

   How for their worth, fond tears must ever fall !

Alas ! even they who mourned are in the mould.

   Asking the tears they gave ! Here " great and small"

Are gathered to one grave—where Palestine   30

Hath strewn its dust—their sepulchre and shrine !

CXII.

These urns are eloquent!—The solemn air

   Breathes deep devotion:—worldly thoughts retire—

Man's passions and pursuits:—joy and despair

   Hushed 'mid the ashes of the funeral pyre!

Beauty and valour—wit and worth are there!—

   The tuneless bard beside his broken lyre!—

All meet at last!—birth, talent, youth, and age,

Barter for rest, life's fever'd heritage!—

CXIII.

Pisa, the peaceful!   Well that epithet

   Becomes thee: Peace is shrined within thy walls

And Plenty crowns thy plain: here I forget

   The world, and all that worldly mind enthrals.

Thy bright Lung' Arno leaves me small regret

   For busier life, or fashion's crowded halls!

To thee consigned—this living solitude

Reclaims the thoughtless—and confirms the good!

CXIV.

PISA, the peaceful! on this laurelled mount,

   With palm-trees sheltering my pavilion round:

In front, a fair stream laughing from its fount,

   And trellised walls, with rose and myrtle bound,

I take my rest; and from my lattice count

   A hundred hills with happy dwellings crowned;—

Hope from thy sky—health with thy breeze inhale

And bless the sun that gladdens ARNO'S VALE!

END OF CANTO FIRST.

CASSANO.

CASSANO.

A CALABRIAN BALLAD.

———

Nel lasciar l'Adda natio
  Se di Russia io tornerò,
Ei le disse—Idolo mio!
  Fido Sposo a te sarò!—

" Adieu! my heart's betrothed !"
  Sighed Cassano's noble son:
" For love of thee I've loathed
  Even the pomp that war has won!
But the vows that I have sworn thee,
  No change can ever know:
And the love that I have borne thee
  Shall bless me where I go!

" My heart is in thy keeping—
  But one more bright campaign !
Then farewell war and weeping,
  And welcome home again !
The song shall wake through Puglia;
  And love, surviving strife,
Shall wing me back to Julia—
  The lodestar of my life !"—

Now sighs and tears were springing
　　Love's soothing could not check ;
Till her fair fond arms unwringing
　　Dropt feebly from his neck:
" Farewell !" she sighed, " and cherish
　　Thoughts of thy hapless bride !
For whom 'twere less to perish
　　Than thus to quit thy side." . . . .

The parting pang is over—
　　The marshalled ranks moved on:
At their haughty head, the lover
　　In his youthful honours shone.
While she, like some fair statue
　　Of her own Sicilian land,
Stood cold and pale, but beautiful,
　　As from the sculptor's hand !

But the bugle sounded cheerily—
　　Their banners gaily dance :
In marshal trim and merrily
　　March forth the arms of France !
Ausonia's land of summer
　　For glory they forego—
To freeze at last, beneath the blast
　　Of Zembla's dreary snow !

*　*　*

Six weary weeks had vanished
   'Twixt hope and hopelessness;
While the bloom of youth was banished
   In the depth of her distress!
At last fresh hopes were granted!—
   When the brilliant *bulletin*
Of splendid trophies vaunted,
   From the Danube to the Seine!

There, the Saxon host was humbled
   At the Eagle-flag's advance!
Here, the Prussian forts had crumbled
   To the fiery touch of France!—
Till the glorious sun of Austerlitz
   Set red in Russian blood;
And the Gallic host, all masterless,
   Swept over field and flood.

And Julia's eye grew starrier,
   When, through its tears of light,
The name of her young warrior
   Stood foremost in the fight!—
She hung her heart's fond offering
   Where the sainted tapers burn:
Her prayers and vows still proffering
   For her true-love's safe return!—

F

The first before the altar,
  The last to leave the shrine;
Her earthly trust might falter—
  But not her trust divine!
Her fancy heard him breathing
  Sweet sounds to his guitar:
While love and hope were wreathing
  His welcome from the war!
              *   *   *

But hark! with brand and buckler—
  And maddening from his fear,
The Russ, so late a truckler,
  Hath poised his Cossack spear!
And now like vultures swooping
  On the straggling host of France,
Dark ruthless hordes are trooping
  With brand and barbed lance!

The prey turns on its beagles—
  The pursuer is pursued!
Yon proud and pampered eagles
  Cower like the turtle's brood!
Bright, bright, but valedictory
  The laurels treasured there!
Their sun, that rose in victory,
  Is lowering in despair!—

Where the *Berezina*'s water
  Rolls o'er the young and brave,
And the wreck of many a slaughter
  Sleeps soundly in its wave:
Where droops the weeping willow
  O'er the Conqueror's shattered car,
And buried 'neath its billow
  The blood-red arm of war:—

There, cheeks that love had chosen,
  And hearts that love had bless'd!
Lay scattered, maimed, and frozen,
  Far, far, from hallow'd rest!
There the shell and shot were showered
  On the Gaul's bewildered flight!
And her starry legions cowered
  In their helplessness of might!

The frown of heaven hung o'er them—
  The curse of earth behind!
A frozen world before them—
  And death in every wind!
Those squadrons fame so flattered!
  Where now their proud array?
Dismembered, maimed, and scattered,
  Like icicles they lay!

'Twas not that Valour failed them—
   But Famine's vulture fang
With gnawing worm assailed them—
   Life's energies unstrang!
Despair their strength had broken—
   The breeze congealed their blood!
And Hope's last lingering token
   Was—to stem that wintry flood!

Then brother called on brother—
   And feebly, through the storm,
The orphan called its mother
   To shield its helpless form!
The veteran sank despairing—
   For here availed not him
His youth's heroic daring—
   Nor strength of heart nor limb!

To men in arms, even death has charms
   On Freedom's battle field,
The slain shall sleep where patriots weep—
   Thrice honoured and annealed!
On the bright fields of his fathers—
   The harvest fields of strife,
Each gallant spirit gathers
   A glory more than life!

But with death like this before him,
  To leave no name behind !—
Thrilled with electric horror
  Through the hapless soldier's mind.
No fame he builds, like that which gilds
  The patriot's lofty brow !—
And on that brink how sad to think
  Such hearts must perish now !

Then wildly on its border
  The weak clung to the strong,
Till down, in dread disorder,
  They rushed—a sinking throng !
The wail was loud—but winter's shroud
  Soon hushed them in its fold—
Where, rank by rank, they shrieked and sank,
  The wounded with the bold !

The *Cossack* gives no quarter,
  The river gives a grave !
Alike await each martyr,
  The sabre or the wave !—

* * *

When months were fled, a stranger
 Stood at Cassano's gate;
With famine worn, and danger,
 And wounds of recent date:
Like one o'ercome with labour,
 And weak from wasted blood;
Supported on his sabre
 The silent stranger stood.

Is none to recognise thee.
 Faint and forgotten one?
That voiceless home denies thee
 A welcome to thine own?
One—only *one* hath started
 That pilgrim step to greet:
His dog, the faithful hearted,
 Is fawning at his feet!

His welcome whine, upbraided.
 The colder heart of man!
Tho' maimed, and worn, and faded,
 His master he could scan!
And now they gathered round him;
 Each look on him was bent:
But oh! how changed they found him,
 From the fair youth that went!

He gazed on them—then shrinking
   With hurried fearful breath—
The earth beneath him sinking—
   In his ear the dream of death!
He spoke—they hid their faces,
   And wiped the silent tear:—
He looked—they showed the traces
   Of a green and recent bier!

They brought him a sweet blossom—
   Its orphan flower just blown:
They placed it on his bosom—
   " 'Tis thine," they said, " thine own!
Thine own—love's first, last token—
   Where a mother scarce had smiled
Till life's silver cord was broken
   As she blessed her new-born child!"

On every infant lineament
   Her image is impressed,
And from those voiceless lips there went
   A deep thrill to his breast!
Pangs sharper than the sharpest sword—
   Feelings till then unknown—
Deep sympathies their torrent poured—
   "Thou'rt mine," he cried, " mine own!"

They led him where she slumbered :—
    He watered with his tears
The marble cross that numbered
    The brief span of her years!
And there these words were written :—
    " O weep not, Love, for me,
That hand our hopes hath smitten
    Hath gifts in store for thee!

" Live—if thou livest!—forget not*
    That heart whose every breath
Was thine!—the love that set not
    But soothed my soul in death.
And, living! if thou findest
    A flower resembling me,
Oh, then to *her* thy love transfer—
    Whose love will comfort thee!

" Hope in my heart had striven
    That thou wouldst bless her birth—
Vain hope! . . . We'll meet in heaven
    Who meet no more on earth!"

     * Immatura perì: sed tu felicior, annos
      Vive tuos, conjux optime, vive meos!

NOTES TO CANTO I.

1.

From Ortegal's bluff headlands, &c.

The well-known cape and castle on the north coast of Gallicia.

2.

With cheek unchafed by the fierce Tramontan.

The Tramontana, a wind prevalent at this season. *La Bise*. Aquilo, Rovajo, Ventavolo of Italians.

2.

Yon scaly brood, led by Leviathan.

The phenomenon here mentioned is familiar to most voyagers on this coast—more particularly at the return of fine weather after a storm. The term *leviathan*, it may be observed, is not employed here in its *restricted* sense.

3.

. . . . On the Pilgrim glancing
Rich and romantic landscapes glimmered near.

The allusion in the text refers more particularly to the tract of coast, comprehending *Hieres* and *Nice*, and which, for beauty and magnificence, is, by the concurring testimony of almost all travellers' unrivalled.

4.

. . . . *Monaco's gray pyramid.*

The capital of a diminutive, but ancient principality; about ten or fifteen miles from Nice—its territory is covered with olives, the source of its prosperity.

> Son Monaco, sopr'uno scoglio,
> Non semino, non recoglio;
> Eppure, mangiar voglio!

5.

. . . . . . *That delicious clime*
Wherein the immortal aloe loves to bloom.

It is almost impossible to do justice to the ever-varying beauty and fertility which distinguish this part of the coast:—

> Partout on voir murir, partout en voit éclore
> Et les fruits de Pomone, et les présens de Flore!

6.

. . . . . . *St. Remo's bell.*

St. Remo, in addition to the merits here recorded, is the birth-place of the famous astrologer, Nostradamus, and contains the celebrated triumphal arch and mausoleum, built by the Romans—still nearly perfect, and much admired by antiquarians.

7.

. . . . . . *Beyond in purple light,*
Proud Genoa soars—a glad and gorgeous sight!

The first view of Genoa, on a morning like the present, seemed nothing less than a work of enchantment. Those only who have seen can form a just estimate of its novel and accumulated beauties; but any description worthy of the subject, will, it is feared, be a hopeless *desideratum* in the pen and portfolio sketches of modern times:—

> Ecco! vediam la maestosa immensa
> Città! che al mar' le sponde, il dorso ai monti
> Occupa tutta, e tutta a cerchio adorna!

8.

And veil flung white from her hair's glossy coil,
Announce the Circé of Liguria's soil!

The dress of the Genoese ladies is peculiarly graceful, and the tasteful disposition of the *mezzaro*, here alluded to, shews the wearer to advantage—particularly at vespers.

9.

While yon Madonna, &c.

In the church of Santo Sirio—a *chef-d'œuvre* of its kind, but still inferior to that in the *Albergo dei Poveri*—the unrivalled work of Michael Angelo.

10.

. . . . . . *Domes that burn*
In molten gold like Nero's.

i. e. Like NERO's golden house of antiquity—not the modern Signor Nero, who has also a palace here. The *dome* alluded to is that in the palace of *Durazzo*, which is entirely covered with *Peruvian* gold burnished!

11.

. . . . . *Treasures amassed*
Were nobly lavished—Charity took root, &c.

For the number and costly magnificence of her charitable institutions and edifices, Genoa stands unrivalled. The *Allergo dei Poveri*,
built and endowed at the expense of a single family—the Brignoli—
is the astonishment of every traveller.

12.

The Doria's sculptured halls are desolate, &c.

The description in the text is to be taken *literally*, and, indeed,
the author is not aware that in any stanza he has greatly, if at all,
diverged through poetical licence, from the real and present state of
Genoa. Those who would know more, and hear worse, have only to
converse with the inhabitants.

13.

. . . . *City of Delight.*

An epithet of endearment by which the Genoese recognise their
capital, and expressive of an affection, such as the Moors still cherish
for their beloved Alhambra.

14.

. . . . . . *Upon the Alpine snow*
A rosy flood survives the parent day.

A phenomenon of imposing splendour, frequent here, and peculiarly enhanced by the immediate vicinity of the sea.

15.

From yon lone shrine, perched on the silent hill, &c.

A place of pilgrimage, crowning the summit of a picturesque hill overlooking the sea.

16.

Here first a school-boy o'er the waters blue,
His future slave, the world's great mariner, &c.

Columbus was born at Genoa in 1447. See "*Vita di Christoforo Colombo, &c. del Cav. Bossi;*" an interesting and well accredited work.

17.

White temples lift their patriarchal towers,
The pilot's landmark and the pilgrim's guide.

This is but another feature of the numberless beauties, which, at every step on this coast, and in endless combinations, excite and keep alive the traveller's admiration.*

18.

There solemn capuchin with cowl and cord.

This, like other religious orders, has had its strength considerably reinforced since the cessation of hostilities; but it appears that many of the brotherhood, though excellent soldiers, make very indifferent capuchins. The present redundancy in the latter, as well as in that of St. Francis, offers melancholy evidence of the state of the country, where, among many of the young nobility, the monastic habit and cell are objects of ambition.

---

* For a very animated and graphic picture of this coast, see Dr. J. Johnson's "Change of Air."

19.

Fettered and goaded creeps the galley slave.

A recent occurrence—and the hero, it is said, of noble family, but afterwards a *carbonaro ;* and, at the time of his capture, a chief of brigands.

20.

And now my steps are on Hetruria's hills.

The road from Genoa to Florence commands an uninterrupted succession of all those varieties of scenery, soil, and productions, for which Italy is so remarkable. The road from Genoa to the Tuscan frontier is of recent and magnificent construction. What scenery and what splendid skies are these!

21.

The banished Danté.

Exulem a Florentia excepit Ravenna, vivo fruens, mortuum colens —tumulum pretiosum musis, S. P. Q. Rav : jure ac ære suo tamquam thesaurum suum munivit, instauravit, ornavit. *Epitaph.*

22.

. . . . . *Even our divinest Bard.*

Milton.—His passionate admiration of Tuscany and Tuscan institutions enters into the subject of many of his epistles. In after life they became the source of many soothing reminiscences—" Were I to open my eyes once more on earth," said he, "I would wish to open them on Fiesolè and the Val d'Arno."
See his Epiatphium Damonis, l. 129.

23.

The dazzling tracks of ether trod alone,
Till the bright vision overwhelmed his own!

This is not merely *poetical.*   Galileo, during his labours upon the telescope, which he brought to unprecedented perfection, and by incessant application to study, and the improvement of his glasses, became blind.

24.

.   .   .   .   *The spell-bound Alfieri.*

In allusion to some characteristic passages in his early and after life, for which see his personal memoirs.

25.

Hither, from colder climes, thy smile to share, &c.

The author's observations on this head are reserved for a subsequent portion of the work. The best books for an invalid are those of Dr. CLARK and Dr. JOHNSON.

26.

She—like the almond-tree, all prematurely
Bursting in flower, &c.

This simile being—as far as the author is acquainted—*new,* is employed with diffidence; although to him its application in the present instance is strikingly characteristic.

27.

Invites repose, and cheers the pilgrim's dream.

The *right* bank, or lungarno, is that recommended as a winter residence for invalids: the *left* bank is exposed to a cold wind from the Apennines.

28.

. . . . . *Yon miraculous Tower.*

The celebrated *leaning tower*, which commands one of the most enchanting views in Italy.—For its history, see *Simond's Travels.*

29.

The Campo-Santo—City of the Dead?

The famous Cemetery of Pisa. See Eustace, Simond, &c.

30.

. . . . . *Where Palestine*
Hath strewn its dust—

It is calculated that, to form this Cemetery, as much earth was imported from the Holy Land by the Pisans (on their return from the third Crusade) as would be a sufficient cargo for fifty vessels of 300 tons burden.

END OF THE NOTES TO CANTO FIRST.

CANTO SECOND.

Canta il prigione, e men molesta e grave,
　　Senta la stretta sua custodia antiça———

Così non per aver gloria, nè vanto,
　　Ma per temprare il duol....io canto.
　　　　　　　　　GIO. L. SEMPRONIO.

ARGUMENT.

CANTO SECOND.

INTRODUCTORY Stanzas—Lyric verses at sea—Present and retro-spective scenes—The modern and ancient Romans—Civita Vecchia—The Tyber—ROME—Sketch of the scenery—Impressions—Approach to Naples—Procida Ischia, &c.—Sketch from the gulf—Neapolitan proverbs—Peculiarities of soil and situation—Traits, physical and moral—Scenes on the Toledo and the Môle—Improvisatore—Achaian tombs—Ancient warrior—Posilippo—VIRGIL's tomb—Impressions in POMPEII— Descriptive stanzas — Eumachia—HERCULANEUM—Descent and description—Lava bust—Apostrophe—Man—His frailty and presumption — BAIÆ — Avernus — Acheron — Sibyl's grotto—Elysian fields — PLINY — LUCULLUS — NERO—Linternum—SCIPIO AFRICANUS—Evening on Misenum —Puteoli—St. PAUL—*Tramon-tana*—Episode—Creed, Christian—Epictetic—Evening in Naples—Symptoms—Volcano — Eruption of VESUVIUS—Scene on the bay during the night—The coral-fisher—Morning—Strange transitions—Characteristic traits—Funeral obsequies and resuscitation—Tomb of CONRAD of Swabia—CAPREÆ—TIBERIUS—Sketch of the island—Apostrophe—Possidonia, PÆSTUM—Sorrento—Evening—Fire-flies—Glow-worm—Apostrophe—Intellectual mind—The fate of Poets—Contrasts—Exhortations—Hygëia—Moral reflexions—Man, his nature and destination—The pilgrim's philosophy in reference to himself—Midnight on the bay of Sorrento—Conclusion.

ERRATUM.

Stanza CIV., p. 51., line 8., for " *Unfolding*," read " *Unfading*."

THE

HELIOTROPE.

CANTO SECOND.

. . . . dulcis alebat
Parthenope.   Virg.

Magni tumulis adcanto Magistri.—Stat.

I.

Is not the world before me?—sunbright shores

   Where scarce a cloud obtrudes'twixt earth and heaven;

Where Flora revels, and Pomona pours

   Spontaneous harvests:—where to man is given

Earth's richest gifts, and art's concentred stores—

   Sage laws—paternal sway: where kings have thriven

And throned in triumph, left their names to be   1

Proud synonymes of immortality.

B

II.

Is not the world before me, where to soothe

This feverish thirst of change ? where I may bound

My wish by Nature's bounty—gently smooth

My footsteps with the flowers that blossom round ?

No—haunted by a spell that mocks at truth—

Hope lures me on—still points to some new ground

More blessed—to skies more balmy still—where time

Sits on the heart, like sunshine on the clime !

III.

Weary of that we have—of that we want

Impatient : led by longings that sum up

Life's brittle span ; one point attained, we pant

With some new enterprise—flavour life's cup

With nectar, that anticipates the plant

Destined to yield it ; ever hungering sup

On shadowy banquet—fever in his veins,

The Pilgrim ever longs for fresher plains.

IV.

Still sympathizing with the changeful hues

    That tinge his mind's horizon—Nature's face,

So beauteous yesterday—to-day imbues

    His soul with mystic gloom; a morbid trace

Sombres the sky; from every healing juice

    He wrings a poison; pines for change of place—

Dwells on each form of unsubstantial joy—

But while he grasps the treasure, finds the alloy!

V.

Sick of no " medicable wound," the mind,

    From her cramp'd tenement, expatiates far

Through Fancy's realms; and in her flight, behind

    Leaves present care, to feign some kindly star,

Within whose bright and magic circle shrined

    Health shall be found, and hush'd the grating jar

Of human passions! Thus, like rainbow skies,

The vision glows, but while he follows, flies!—

1.

But now the main—the heaving main—
  The world of waves before me !
In evening shades, Hetruria fades—
  New stars are kindling o'er me !
Again I breathe, where the billows seethe,
  And the breeze dispels my sadness !
When thoughts be dark, oh, what like the bark,
  Can change my grief to gladness !

2.

No scene for me like the bounding sea !
  No couch like my cabin pillow !
No fair domain like yon ocean's plain,
  And my coursers—the breeze and billow !
Then on, still on, where Nature's zone
  And the looks of love are brightest !
Where the groves are green, and the sky serene,
  And the breath of heaven the lightest !

3.

Where song and summer, meeting, gild
    The land with two-fold glory!
And every cliff, that greets my skiff,
    Detains me with its story!
Thus let me roam, till I find a home
    Which health and beauty hallow!
In bowers of spring, here rest my wing;
    Then change, and choose like the swallow!

VI.

The breath of morn is on the blue Tyrrhene:
    Elba behind; and, shadowed in the water,
What classic grandeur marks the opening scene,
    As history counts her ancient fields of slaughter!—
Her tombs, towers, aqueducts, and temples green
    Bordering the shore! where still LATINUS' daughter
Sits throned in song—the Trojan at her side,—
And baffled TURNUS battles for his bride! 3

VII.

Here trophied fragments of antiquity

    Obstruct the plough; there Parian sculpture paves

The unpeopled street, or stems the encroaching sea:

    Yet, 'mid those columns tottering o'er the graves

Of Latian kings, their haughty progeny

    Stand proudly forth; and—pointing to the waves—

The sky and clime—their temples and their towers—

Exclaim with patriot pride—These—these are ours!   4

VIII.

Our heritage! then deem ye we are poor,

    Weighing our glory, balanced with your gold?

Ours is the wealth that gives the Italian boor

    A noble's patent! Though oppressed and sold—   5

Though commerce starves, where fleets were wont to moor

    Freighted with plenty!—*we* are not grown cold,

Nor callous: but with hearts thus disunited,

Our strength, like our volcanic soil, is blighted!

IX.

What sank the Babylonian, and the Mede,

    Persian, and Greek, and last our Roman realm?

Disunion!—jealousies—the jarring creed

    Of sordid int'rests! Traitors at the helm

And slaves to row—the galley hath small need

    Of storms, or Jove's forked thunder to o'erwhelm

Her prosperous course:—of winds and waves the sport,

The Syrtis is her shore—Charybdis is her port!   6

X.

But that which made, would make us still, man's dread

    Or his defence—is the strong heart and arm

Of Concord! Let *her* but exalt her head,   7

    Where now her deep-based temple stands—hearts warm,

Hands willing—patriots worthy of the dead

    And Rome's best day—forth starting at the charm

Of her lost voice!—regenerated bloom

Should fill the land, and change our moral doom!

XI.

Yes !—phœnix-like, from out their scattered pyres

   Romans should spring to vindicate that name

And spirit, which (now spent in poor desires—

   Pursuits that scarce a Sybaris would claim !)

Once roused and swayed the Senate's ancient sires—

   Winged their swift edicts—made their favour *fame*—

Their consuls kings ! their curule chair a throne—

Their sages demi-gods—the world their own !

      * * *

XII.

But lo, the Tyber ! Distant, yet not dim,   8

   The Eternal City glimmers from her hills :

And brightly skirting the horizon's rim,

   Albano conjures up, Frescati fills

The mind with glorious images that swim

   Embodied on my gaze ! There gushing rills—

Groves evergreen : with evening sapphires warm,

Here smiles Soracté—there the " Sabine Farm !"

XIII.

Tombs sentinel the plain—itself a tomb,

That undulates with dust! each lofty mole

Whose arches rise like triumphs o'er the doom

Of empire—in whose channels rivers roll—

Causeways that drain the distant hills in Rome!   9

All wake unwonted feelings in the soul

And draw me on, where, glorious in her fall,

Earth's mighty mistress spreads her gorgeous pall.

XIV.

No Tully fulmines in her forum now!   10

No fire in Vesta's fane! Her Capitol

Is but a shrine, where pilgrims pause to bow

Over her relics! Withered like a scroll

Of cypress, clings the laurel to her brow!

And where the car of triumph wont to roll

Through captive kings—miasma taints the gale

And the maimed arch hath half forgot its tale!

XV.

But here I trespass.   Now, fair Procida—   11
   And Ischia (piled on rebel giant's limbs!)
Show their volcanic clefts; while Nisita
   Robed in her own immortal summer, swims
Like Nereid-palace, buoyant on the Bay.
   Transparent round Vesuvio's crater skims
The sulphurous vapour—white as Alpine snow
Sorrento spreads her palaced shore below!

XVI.

Aloof, old Capri's castellated rocks
   O'erlook the wave; Misenum sentinels
His Trojan relics; leeward, Baiæ locks
   The bright wave in her bosom; proudly swells
St. Elmo, frowning from his lava blocks:
   Beneath—the " city of a thousand spells,"
Set like a precious gem —PARTHENOPĒ
Smiles as of yore—the Syren of the sea!   12

XVII.

The world is now before me, where to chuse
   My peaceful sojourn.   There Sorrento greets
Me welcome, with the voice of Tasso's muse !   13
   Here Posilippo from her laurelled seats,
Points to the Sepulchre, where Genius strews
   Her votive garland ! There, thy cool retreats,
Camaldoli ! Each with a Syren's voice
That breathes enchantment round me.—Take thy choice !

XVIII.

Here are the shades that cradled young Romance—
   That realize the poet's wildest dream !
Where, breathing gladness, sea-born Zephyrs dance ;
   And glittering towns in fairy prospect gleam :
Where groves of spices woo thee to advance ;
   And arched with rainbows from its fount the stream
Dashing descends, or musically slow,
Pours its spring beverage o'er the vale below.

XIX.

" Look but on Naples," say her bards, "and die,"   14

    Or, living, never hope to see again

Campania's garden, or Salerno's sky !—

    So rich in all that maketh monarchs vain—

That schools the sage, or fires the poet's eye !

    And sooth to say, who sees her will retain

In his mind's eye a gorgeous soil, and clime,

The last to vanish with the lapse of time !

XX.

They tell me 'tis a "fragment dropt from heaven !"

    Whose flowers, perennial fruits, and perfumes sprung

From roots in Paradise, ere man was driven

    In exile from its bowers—with bosom stung,

By guilt and sorrow, till these shores were given

    In lieu of his lost Eden !—Yet, though flung

From heaven thus richly fraught—still, as of yore,

The Tempter sows hot discord through its core !

XXI.

And, torn by the fierce conflict, like man's breast,

  By struggling passions, this electric soil   15

Shows her hot scars, and from the mountain's crest

  To the sea-shore, the ravage and turmoil

Of hostile elements, have deep impressed

  Her surface with revolt: dense caldrons boil—

The insidious furnace burns—the seething lake

Vomits hot vapour—'mid the flowery brake!

XXII.

Questioned—the impassive earth replies with flame;

  The mountains feed, and, simmering, the broad bay 16

Heaves o'er, a forge! Convulsed through all her frame

  Earth burns, yet is not blighted: lightnings play—

Red rolls the lava tide, but cannot tame

  Down to sterility her teeming clay!

Though scathed to-day—to-morrow, from its tomb,

Her verdure springs with renovated bloom!

XXIII.

Here in their beds of lava, cities sleep :   17

   And hills heaved from the earth's hot bosom soar

Where cities flourished !—Even yon peopled steep

   Stands piled on fire, that strains to burst its core,

Whose brittle crust alone debars the deep

   Dread vortex from its streets !   Yet evermore

Life crowds the spot ! men laugh, and leave their saint

To avert the judgments gloomier spirits paint !

XXIV.

And living while they live, do they not well ?

   Their life's a banquet; and while sages make

Their couch on ashes, and by learning swell

   Death's startling chances !—*they*, incredulous, quake

With no prophetic horrors !   Where they dwell,

   Their fathers dwelt, and died, and shall awake !

That love which binds Helvetia's mountaineer,

'Mid rocks and snows, glows in the lava here !

XXV.

With life these streets o'erflow—exuberant

   As is their soil :—there ranged the gaudy stalls

Well piled with fruit, and glittering traffic, plant

   Their motley ensigns ; Pulcinello calls

His faithful votaries ; Cappucini chant   18

   Their Lady's hymn ; Calabria's bagpipe squalls—

Monks rant, empirics bawl ; in pilgrim weeds

The bandit tells his plunder with his beads !

XXVI.

There masked processions bear the unmasked dead ;

   Here pious sisters chant lugubrious olio ;

Scribes write, knaves plead, and lazzaroni spread

   Nets for the novice ; near the shrined *rosoglio*

The thirsty take their stand ; the bay's calm bed

   Gleams like a rich illuminated folio !   19

While, over all Vesuvius spouts his fire ;

And fitful thunders thrill the electric wire.

XXVII.

Yonder, in lazy groups along the Mole,

   An old grey minstrel binds the listening crowd

With the strong bond of passion; numbers roll

   Sonorous from his lips; pompous and loud

He tells the Tale of Troy; scanty in stole,—

   But rich in a rude harp—humble yet proud

Of his high calling—the Improvisatoré   20

Recites the startling page of ancient story!

XXVIII.

And see, the circle narrows, as the tale

   Reaches its climax; or the antithesis

Well pointed strikes: how Ammon's wasting hail

   Levelled the cities! How the bowers of bliss,

Tempted by sons of Earth, beheld them quail

   To the dread Thunderer! With such theme as this,

He sways the mob, revives their patriot fires,

Then points in triumph to the gods, their sires!

XXIX.

Here, in the pilgrim's ear, the Achaian tombs
    Scooped in the height and hollowed on the shore,
Tell their first history: while the aloe blooms—
    The palm tree blossoms, as in days of yore—
The blue bay laves, and the same sky illumes
    The land of their renown; and where ye pore
With curious eye, lodged in their pristine fanes,
    Behold the dust that once adorned those plains!

XXX.

There, housed with his old armour and his god,
    The warrior slumbers: that wherein he trusted
Still guards his grave, and from the hallowed clod
    Proclaims how prowess, with his creed adjusted,
Left him a sovereign, where the exile trod;
    But now his gods, frail as his glaive, are rusted,
Shrineless and fallen! nations round him rise
That know not him nor his divinities!

c

XXXI.

Yet, where their sepulchres rise by the sea,   21

    Whose land they loved, adopted, and adorned,

Calm let them rest! nor shame their sanctuary

    By sordid pillage; but, where they were mourned,

Or mourners and retired to their long rest—

    As we must all!—with feelings unsuborned

By cold research,—sift not the little spoil,

That nature spares them from its kindred soil!

*   *   *

XXXII.

Sweet Posilippo! 'mid thy cedared swell   22

    And sunny gardens, art and nature meet.

In rival lustre! Here how sweet to dwell,

    Girt by the scenes of yore! and, at my feet,

Hear Amphitrité tune her murmuring shell,

    And music melt from every green retreat!

Gazing on thee, the pilgrim's fancy sees

The golden shades of old Hesperides!

XXXIII.

Following the votive path, winding, half hid
　　With laurel and pomegranate leaves, they show
A sacred pile—a time-worn pyramid
　　Festooned with many flowers—Who sleeps below?
Behold the name! and let the distich bid
　　Thee bow before it! mocking time's dull flow
And moral darkness—here the Aonian choir
Still lingering guard the Master's broken lyre!　　23

XXXIV.

The Poet's song, and sanctifying dust,
　　Here left, and living, stamp upon the soil
The seal of immortality! though bust
　　Nor monument of man's elaborate toil,
Nor precious bronze, nor sculptured urn incrust
　　The haunted precincts—what time cannot spoil,
Nor man impair—traits of immortal mind
Claim for that dust the homage of mankind!

c 2

XXXV.

Here, every tree and stone have found a tongue !

   Here, rapture-smit, Boccacio, for the lyre,   24

Renounced the world !—inspired by him who sung

   The Trojan Exile—woes and warfare dire—

How Latium rose, and fair Lavinium sprung

   A second Ilium !   Oh, how poor the pyre

That kingdoms raise ! how poor the Cæsars' sway,

To his, whose empire was the Epic lay !

       *   *   *

XXXVI.

Pompeia ! disentombed Pompeia ! Here   25

   Before me in her pall of ashes spread—

Wrenched from the gulf of ages—she whose bier

   Was the unbowelled mountain, lifts her head

Sad, but not silent !   Thrilling in my ear

   She tells her tale of horror, till the dread

And sudden drama mustering through the air,

Seems to rehearse the day of her despair !

XXXVII.

Joyful she feasted 'neath her olive tree,

    Then rose to " dance and play:" and if a cloud

O'ershadowed her thronged circus, who could see

    The impending deluge brooding in its shroud ?

On went the games ! mirth and festivity

    Increased—prevailed : till rendingly and loud

The earth and sky with consentaneous roar

Denounced her doom—that time should be no more !

XXXVIII.

Shook to its centre, the convulsive soil

    Closed round the flying :—Sarno's tortured tide   26

O'erleapt its channel—eager for its spoil !

    Thick darkness fell, and, wasting fast and wide,

Wrath opened her dread floodgates !   Brief the toil

    And terror of resistance :—art supplied

No subterfuge !—the pillared crypt, and cave

That proffered shelter, proved a living grave !   27

XXXIX.

Within the circus, tribunal, and shrine,

   Shrieking they perished : there the usurer sank   28

Grasping his gold ; the bacchant at his wine ;

   The gambler at his dice ! age, grade, nor rank,

Nor all they loved, revered, or deemed divine,

   Found help or rescue ; unredeemed they drank

Their cup of horror to the dregs, and fell

With heaven's avenging thunders for their knell !

XL.

Their city a vast sepulchre !—their hearth   29

   A charnel house !   The beautiful and brave,

Whose high achievements, or whose charms, gave birth

   To songs, and civic wreath, unheeded crave

A pause 'twixt life and death : no hand on earth,

   No voice from heaven, replied to close the grave

Yawning around them.   Still the burning shower

Rained down upon them with unslackening power !

XLI.

'Tis an old tale !   Yet, gazing thus, it seems
  But yesterday the circling wine-cup went   30
Its joyous round !   Here still the pilgrim deems
  New guests arrive—the reveller sits intent
At his carousal—quaffing to the themes
  Of Thracian Orpheus : lo, the cups indent
The conscious marble, and the amphoræ still
Seem redolent of old Falerno's hill !

XLII.

It seems but yesterday !   Half sculptured there,
  On the paved forum wedged, the marble shaft
Waits but the workman to resume his care,
  And reed it by the cunning of his craft.   31
The chips, struck from his chisel, fresh and fair,
  Lie scattered round ; th' acanthus leaves ingraft
The half-wrought capital ; and Isis' shrine
Retains untouched her implements divine.   32

XLIII.

The streets are hollowed by the rolling car

   In sinuous furrows ; there the lava stone

Retains, deep grooved, the frequent axle's scar.   33

   Here oft the pageant passed, and triumph shone;

Here warriors bore the glittering spoils of war,

   And met the full, fair city smiling on

With wreath and pæan !—gay as those who drink

The draught of pleasure on destruction's brink !

XLIV.

The frescoed wall, the rich mosaic floor,

   Elaborate, fresh, and garlanded with flowers

Of ancient fable :—crypt, and lintelled door   34

   Writ with the name of their last tenant—towers

That still in strength aspire, as when they bore

   Their Roman standard—from the whelming showers

That formed their grave—return, like spectres risen,

To solve the mysteries of their fearful prison !

XLV.

Eumachia ! last fair relic of that shrine   35
   Where—once a worshipper—half worshipped now,
Thy presence hallows what was then divine.
   Those features how celestial ! on that brow
What dignity ! Was ever beauty's line
   More sweetly moulded ! Well may pilgrim bow—
This is no idol—no idolatry
To give what homage Pallas claimed, to *thee !*

XLVI.

It seems as if the very stone that wears
   Thy living semblance, had survived the hour
That strewed the fane, to shed through after years
   A lingering sanctity—a mystic dower—
Around that altar !—So, where Beauty rears
   Her sceptre—man still moulded to her power,
Will render homage with impassioned breast,
And deem each spot divine her presence bless'd.

XLVII.

But lo, the " street of sepulchres," where bust,   36

   And scroll, and epicede, and cenotaph,

And urns with pristine ashes !—human dust

   Which that dread day, that turned their fields to chaff—

Their city to a shroud—spared in its crust

   Inviolate ; while their wretched children—half

Of that fair province ! blasted in their pride,

Sank down unwept—unmonumented died !

XLVIII.

And here the living—while erecting tombs   37

   To shrine ancestral dust—left off their toil

To find their own ! Where now the citron blooms,

   And fig-trees flourish—sifted from the spoil

Of centuries, the mattock still exhumes

   Their urnless relics—where the sacred oil

Was never sprinkled—where the pious tear

Of kindred sorrow, never reached their bier !

*   *   *

XLIX.

And yet more dread seems Heracleïa's doom !

   If, twixt the seething lava, and the shower   38

That whelmed them both, the living may presume

   One fierce alternative in that last hour,

To choose the flood or ashes for their tomb !

   These time unlocks—of that cements the power ;

The ashes' hold, man's labour can unclasp,

But scarce may loose the lava's iron grasp !

L.

The sunset left her basking in its beam,

   Her streets o'erflowing—peace within her wall

" And plenty in her garner ;" when the scream

   Of frenzy wakening with the lava fall

Invoked the gods ! Girt by the smouldering steam

   Of that mephitic flood, the piteous call

Brought but despairing echoes ; till the flow

Of scorching torrents hushed the wail of woe !

LI.

Some shrieked, and fainting, died; others too strong
    To sink without a struggle—struggled hard
For life and those they loved!   But 'twas not long—
    No strength could bar the torrent or retard
Its whelming sweep!   The loftiest dome among
    Their temples, lent but momentary ward.
The torrent scaled the wall—gushed through the gate—
Forced every door—and drove them to their fate!

LII.

Some cursing, called their gods. Some, by the flood   39
    Moulded like statues, stood erect, and flung
Their desperate looks to heaven:—their seething blood
    Shot frenzy through the maddening brain, and stung
Like scorpions—there each writhing victim stood
    Till the red deluge, fiercely deepening, wrung
Him in its grasp; and, quenched, the stiffening flame
Closed like an iron coffin round his frame!

*   *   *

LIII.

Enough—Now let me thread the deep dark cell

    Bored through the lava blocks.   A flickering torch

Brandished by a grim guide, consorteth well

    With the wild scene!   A half unburied porch

Yawns on my right, where yet the breath of hell

    Nauseates the sense that kindled it would scorch!

Deeper and gloomier, my strained eyes explore

The lofty circus, vault, and corridor;   41

LIV.

Farther, and darker, where the pick-axe cleaves

    A path; ghost-like the city, with her gods

Glued by the lava to their shrine, receives

    My faltering step: in chambers once the abodes

Of life and sunshine—where the bronze still heaves

    With human likeness—lo, the miner plods

With torch and mattock, and discoursing, shows

The hoarded fragments of Heraclia's woes!

LV.

And last, he led me to a bust whereon

   Few look unmoved, and, leaving, turn again

To gaze: not sculptured from the Parian stone,

   Nor bronze of Corinth, nor the Theban plain—

But cast, when the fierce lava-flood was thrown

   On living hearts!   A monument of pain

Surpassing thought—where beauty left the mould

Of her soft bosom in its fiery fold!   41

LVI.

It is a sacred relic, taking place

   Of sterner records; hideously acquainting

The eye with woe's extreme !   Behold the face

   Beauteous, then blackening—eloquently painting

Its helpless victim in the fierce embrace

   Of her destroyer—like a demon tainting

Her life's sweet breath—till, withered to the core,

She left her likeness in the burning ore!

LVII.

Yet why pursue the theme ?   Have not since then
   Proud cities been entombed ; and ocean's deep
Paved with the populous abodes of men ?
   True ! but like these, roused from its iron sleep,
What city hath returned to earth again   42
   To meet man's gaze ? None ! and 'tis hence we reap
Strange, thrilling pleasure, as with living tread,
Thus met, we strike life's balance with the dead !

LVIII.

Here, with these walls thy preachers, pause, proud man !
   Thou thing of nothing, yet presuming all ;
And grasping worlds within thy little span :
   A breath consumes thee !—as the sere leaves fall
Thou fallest, with thy deep digested plan
   Of wealth, and power ! As on a fiery ball
The moth expires, thy grandeur is burnt up,
Thy pride abased, and dashed thy pleasure's cup !

LIX.

Poor in thy strength—more lamentably poor

 In thy presumption !— poorest where the crowd

Flatter thee most !   Chaff from the threshing floor

 Rivals thy riches !   Yet thy boast is loud—

Thy port is lofty !   Girt with sordid ore

 Thou scoff'st at heaven !   Like *thee*, such were the proud

Who prospered *here*, where yet the lava street,

That shows their footprints, forms their winding sheet !

LX.

Even thou, who pratest of wisdom, what the extent,

 And depth of thy discerning ?   'Tis to feel

The shallows of research, and the high bent

 Of thy ambition stampt with the dark seal

Of mystery !   What, though thy full years be spent

 In studious toil, what harvest crowns thy zeal ?

Nothing ! the boundless ocean spreads before,

Whilst thou but gatherest weeds upon its shore !   43

* * *

LXI.

Lo, Baia's shore! Avernus! Acheron!—   44

· Cimmerian Cumæ!—and the Leucrine lake!—

The Sibyl's labyrinth, scooped from living stone—

    Each with its stamp and classic tale that wake

Thrilling emotion—conjuring back the tone

    Of ardent boyhood!   Voices from the brake,

The tomb, and temple, greet me: at the sound

I start, and find my steps on haunted ground!

LXII.

Climbing the rocky steep, the Elysian Fields

    Lie stretched before!   How oft in Fancy's hour,

Led by the Mantuan Bard, whose genius wields

    The immortal sceptre of poetic power,

And gives eternity to all it gilds—

    Musing alone, in some sequestered bower,

Have those bright regions peopled with the blessed,

Soothed me with visions of celestial rest!

LXIII.

The song remains—but all unlike the song

   Those fields! where flowered the amaranth, and springing

Melodious fountains murmured through the long

   Delicious avenues ! rank weeds are clinging

To mouldering tombs !   Yon stagnant pools among,

   Stalks the lean stork ; here to the desert singing,

The bittern broods : and, hissing as ye pass,

There, the coiled scorpion glitters in the grass.

LXIV.

Farther, I trace the steps of him whose thirst

   Of nature's mystic lore, made death the price

Of his ambition—PLINY ! not the first

   To pay such forfeit !—Here, refined i ᐧ vice,

His laurels in voluptuous age immersed,—

   His days to pleasure one long sacrifice,—

Lucullus lived to feast and died a fool—

The wealthiest vassal of the Apician school.   45

LXV.

But damp and dreary now the pillared cave,
　　Where, housed, the Aristippus of his time
Hoarded the sensual banquet—when the wave
　　Was dragged—earth ransacked—Afric's burning clime
Taxed for his table : all that wish could crave
　　Or wealth supply—even with the tools of crime—
Glutted his larder !　Oh, by what vile claims,
Wealth mounts to fame and spurns at noble names !

LXVI.

Weed, brier, and thorn usurp the place of kings !
　　The toppling arch, and tesselated bath,
The prostrate column, the lopt eagle's wings,
　　Whose flight was triumph, block the imperial path !
Time-wasted temples—desecrated springs—
　　Serapis—Phœbus—quailing to the wrath
Of foes or ocean's fury—pave the strand
Where BAIÆ stood—the Sybaris of the land !　　46

LXVII.

The pilgrim's bark—the fisher's baited hook—

    Floats o'er and frets the sunk mosaic floor,

Where banqueted those haughty lords who shook

    An empire with their nod, and lavished ore

That would have ransomed kingdoms : every nook

    Displays its relics ! even the blue sea-shore

Sparkles with gems, where, throned on blood and fear !

Rome served her parricide, and charioteer !   47

LXVIII.

But lo, the wave invades his crumbled wall—

    His palace glimmers through the sunny water !

Combing her sea-green locks in NERO's hall

    The mermaid weaves her song to Ocean's daughter !

All that had witnessed, all that might recal

    Those nights of revel, closing days of slaughter, 48

Lie buried—not oblivious—where the flood

Murmurs of him, whose pastime was in blood !

LXIX.

Linternum ! one dilapidated tower—   50

  Thy city's landmark !—leads my steps where he,

The prop, yet victim, of his country's power,

  Lived in lone exile—that he might live free,

Albeit forgotten !   Thus, of his last hour,

  Yon tomb bears record:—" Loving, serving thee !

Ungrateful Rome ! what crowns my patriot toil ?

Long exile ! and a grave in foreign soil !"

LXX.

Yet, let me linger ! loth to quit the height

  So dear to young remembrance, and so beaming

With what no deeds can dim—heaven's holy light,

  And that bright sky—bright as my fondest dreaming

Ere feigned or sighed for ! and with such a night—

  Such mingled charms along the horizon gleaming—

Ischia—Miseno—Baia's bay and hill,

And Capri, make the clime Elysian still !

LXXI.

At such an hour of yore, the Roman sage

   Loitered along these cliffs, or studious viewed

With feelings—such as soothe my pilgrimage,—

   Those scenes and classic solitudes imbued

With Homer's genius—all that charmeth age,

   Or fires the youthful spirit: here renewed

That moral strength and manly power, that swept

The chords of rhetoric till whole senates wept!   51

LXXII.

And now, Puteoli! I turn to thee,   52

   Whose meanest pavement speaks; circus and shrine

Proclaim the pomp of thine antiquity!

   Profusely scattered, as in some rich mine,

From old Serapis' columns to the sea

   Thy gorgeous relics glimmer in the brine:

Thy port a prodigy—thy very clay

Imperishable, as thine Appian Way!

LXXIII.

'Twas here, the mightiest of the Twelve—the man   53

  Whose word made tetrarchs tremble—landing drew

The gentile to his standard, and began

  His Roman work—here met the chosen few

Whom heaven disposed to aid the glorious plan

  Of its high legate—watering as it grew

That plant of power which, strengthened by his hand,

Soon compassed with its boughs the pagan land !

*   *   *

LXXIV.

Heaven's breath is chilled ! The Tramontana's wing   54

  Hath scared Favonius !—nipt the citron's bloom—

Shrivelled the blossom in the lap of Spring—

  And, where it found a garden, leaves a tomb !

Where flowers were sweetest there it loves to fling

  Unkindly frost, transforming joy to gloom—

Pleasure to pain—and, with ungenial breath

Where buds were ripening, shedding hues of death !

LXXV.

So pale Consumption o'er the young fresh cheek

   Breathes desolation! and where hopes were springing—

Pledges that seemed of happy days to speak—

   And round us jocund Health her treasures flinging!

Then forth, like the Simöom fierce and bleak,

   She hastens—from the bough the blossom wringing!

Her victims still the fairest! stricken—dying—

But on their wasted cheek the rose leaves lying!

LXXVI.

Oh, bitter mockery!   Thus life's prospect ends—

   Like day in blushes!—Sad, yet edified

By that stern preacher Death—less foe than friend!

   I've watched the night; where *she*, so late a bride—

So soon a widow! felt that pang which rends

   Strong hearts! and saw the husband of her pride,

Like a brief shadow from the mountain's belt—

Slow vanishing before her where she knelt!

LXXVII.

For him she crossed yon Alps— for him forsook

    Home and its joys; Hope's handmaids strewed the way

With flowers that seemed to ripen; Honour shook

    Her treasures round them : but the brighter day

And balmier whispers of the south wind strook

    No vigour through his frame : still, still Decay

Struck deeper—firmer root; till, sapped at length

Each vital source—slow sank his manly strength !

LXXVIII.

Then, with a soft calm voice, clasping her hand

    He blessed her—blessing Heaven for the brief sum

Of their endearments ; to its last command

    He bowed, nor murmured that his hour was come,

Save that he left her in the stranger's land,

    A stranger ! While he spoke, his lips grew dumb,

His eyes waxed dim—but still he seemed to speak,

And sunrise threw fresh life into his cheek !

LXXIX.

Why wait ye?   Bear the living from the dead—
    The dead to kindred dust !   And if ye weep—
Weep that ye must live on, and living shed
    Fresh tears lamenting him whose tranquil sleep
Needeth no sorrow ! for the oil that fed
    Life's lamp, burnt out, hath called him hence to reap
That which the living cannot reap—repose,
And bliss—if but oblivion of life's woes !

LXXX.

Like a dull stream that purifies by flowing,
    My thoughts flow onward; where I following find
Health in the change—some fresher tint still glowing
    In fair prospective; but man's credulous mind
Leans oft on reeds : and I, though all unknowing
    My future warfare, am not wholly blind
To that which must be :—still, from that which is,
If spring some drops of balm, I count it bliss !

LXXXI.

Formed to enjoy—with longings ill repressed—
   Led by our spirit's law—life's first essay
Is happiness! Still in the future blessed—
   The past forgot—we give our hearts a prey
To expectation! Happier did we rest—
   And if not pleased, yet passive! our brief day
Is quickly summed. Then leave thy hopes and sorrow
To Him who gives—and may withhold—to-morrow!

LXXXII.

Man's best philosophy—life's purest creed—
   Christian as Epictetic—is:—*To bear*   55
Our yoke unmurmuring; balance that we need
   With that which we desire; to bound our prayer
To heaven's good pleasure; make the word and deed
   Our heart's true mirror; on our breasts to wear
Bravely our badge; and if at last we leave
Some trait worth name, what more would man achieve?

*   *   *

LXXXIII.

But hark! the streets are hushed! while to and fro
  Men pass in silence: gathering on the Mole
Like statues, mutely grouped, they watch the glow
  Reflected from the wave; or muffled stroll
Along Chiaja—while denouncing woe
  Vesuvius vomits flame—and thunders roll! `
Can days so beautiful prelude such night,—
Such darkness blot the landscape of delight?

LXXXIV.

The crater is convulsed; the lava-stream   56
  Boils o'er the brim: beneath, the reddening bay
Gleams like a sea of blood: the vesper beam
  Is blotted from the sky;—red meteors play
Far up the flushed horizon!—like the dream
  Of doomsday horrors, closing round their prey—
The sky rains ashes, and the electric cloud,
Hangs o'er the city, like a funeral shroud!

LXXXV.

This is no night for slumber: and with heart
  Thrilled by strange sympathies, I take my seat
On the felucca's bow: Around me start
  Electric ripples as the glimmering sheet
Of the broad basin, fretted like a chart
  With fouldering lightnings, slakes the hissing sleet
Shot from the mountain; where with brandished torch
Tartarean furies feed the bellowing porch!

LXXXVI.

And lo, as if in dread, the Bay is hushed!
  But deep reflecting from her breast the fierce
And startling conflict; darkling, and now flushed
  With crimson streaks, as the fleet lightnings pierce
The asphaltic curtain: rocks to atoms crushed—
  And each a meteor—playfully rehearse
Their horrid game! and from the Thunderer's forge,
In midway heaven their scorching hail disgorge.

LXXXVII.

Down rush the torrents, flashing as they flow,　　　57
　　And, with a force like frantic Scylla's tide,
Scathe all before them : forth their channels throw
　　Mephitic vapours, smouldering as they glide,
Here the live flame, and there the lurid glow—
　　Till the breach forced anew—the mountain's side
Bursts out afresh, and the volcanic shell
Explodes in thunder from its native hell !

LXXXVIII.

Earth trembles to the shock !—Again—again
　　The giant groans in agony, and flashes—
Such as smote down the " Cities of the Plain"—
　　Like hurtling spears alternate with the crashes
Of earth-forged thunder !—headlong cataracts drain
　　The boiling Acheron, through its bleeding gashes
Half flood—half flame—while from the appalling glare
Sorrento shrinks, like beauty in despair !

LXXXIX.

The scene is full of grandeur! dread—sublime
  Beyond or speech, or painting! Who can tell
The lava's limits? Who restrict the time
  And terrors of the storm? Hath not its swell
Already swept fair cities from the clime,
  And launched its thunders for their funeral knell?—
The bolts are forged—their fires have not waxed cold,
And wait but to revive the woes of old!

XC.

Dread sympathy! strike this electric chain,
  The summoned hills reply! Vesuvius calls,
Ætna with sudden deluge sweeps the plain;
  Dark Strombolo lights his volcanic halls:
While, consentaneous, through the secret main,
  Hecla, invoked, o'erleaps her molten walls!
The train is laid—the thunder knows its path
To each dread storehouse, in the day of wrath!

XCI.

Dazzling his vision as on deck he watches—

   Mocking the pale lamp, glimmering at his bows,

Red meteors gleam—the white brailed canvass catches

   The sullen sheen—where, muttering as he rows,

Oft from his breast the coral fisher snatches

   The hoarded relic—safeguard from all woes !

While every flash from the volcano's brim,

Renews the fervour of his vesper hymn !   59

XCII.

But lo, night wanes !   A hand behind the storm

   Bridles its rage: that mystic power which bids

States spring or perish—yet for the blind worm

   Secures a path—has quenched yon pyramid's

Portentous fire —restored to Nature's form

   Her wonted radiance ; and o'er wakeful lids,

Morn breaks with balmy freshness, and a light,

Thrice welcome, when it scares such dismal night !

      *   *   *

XCIII.

And hark, guitar, and song, and tarantella,   60

    Resume their sway, and rule the laughing hour!

And from the high-bred dame to the donzella,

    All feel the change, and yield to pleasure's power!

Betwixt Gennaro's shrine and Pulcinella,

    The crowd divides! Wreathed with his favourite flower

This hath his lamps, and *that* his fame increased,

And fears have vanished in the dance and feast!

XCIV.

Transition strange! Yet here 'tis principle!

    Familiar grown, Death drops his hideous guise;

In human hearts live passions that can quell

    Or scorn his terror: woman's love defies—

Hate braves it:—Mirth, from horror's passing knell,

    Bursts like an unstemmed torrent! Cloudless skies

Give cloudless hearts: subdued while dangers last,

But gone, returning revels drown the past!   61

E

XCV.

How Proteus-like this people !   Every hour
    Processions pass—masks grin ;—grim death uprears
The cross and scutcheon; while the church's power,
    Still measured by her vapid pomp, appears
In her state livery !   Lo, a bier with flower
    And foliage wreathed—moist with a mother's tears—
Halts 'neath my casement !   'Tis a lovely child,
Dead—but still fresh as if in sleep it smiled !   62

XCVI.

So death beneath the rose-bud loves to smile,
    And smiling blasts it !   Yet, was ever death
So like a cherub's sleep ? or left the while
    Such hues outliving the departed breath ?
Dead, but a few brief hours ! they haste to pile
    The cold earth on its cheek !   "Who knows if 'neath
That roseate tint, life may not linger yet,
And be rekindled where it seems to set !"

XCVII.

Who spoke they knew not—but the mourners' look
   Smiled, with mixed scorn and pity, as he raised
The infant's head—chafed its chill hand, and took
   Some mystic balm, and sprinkled as he gazed.
And lo, it moved; life came by starts;—it shook
   Death's garland from its bosom! All amazed,
Exclaimed, " A miracle !" and rushed anon
To canonize the seer—but he was gone!

XCVIII.

Rescued, the slumberer broke his trance's bond
   And sprang to life! The mother shrieked and swooned
In her ecstatic joy! The crowd respond
   With tears and salutations! Now her wound
Is bathed with balm! and she so sad—so fond—
   Hath yet a son! life's sweetest chords retuned
To gladness! And for Death's lugubrious rite
Life, hope, and joy shall be her guests to night!
* * *
E 2

XCIX.

Conrad ! the last of Swabia's line—young—brave—

    By wrongs immortalized !   Oft has thy story   63

Roused indignation's bitter tears !   The glaive

    Of legal murder never did its gory

Office on neck that more had died to save !

    Stranger and kinsman envied thee the glory

Of thy young martyrdom, and made thy tomb

Their pilgrimage—till heaven avenged thy doom !

C.

Here where they raise the expiatory rood—

    An altar on the spot where Conrad fell—

The clay still blushes with his guiltless blood !

    And pauses the gray Sacristan to tell

The tragic tale :—In childless widowhood

    How his sad mother craved some hallowed cell

To keep his ashes !   How they mocked her tears,

And how she was avenged in after years !

*   *   *

CI.

But now the breeze is fair—cross we the brine
   To CAPRI! Yet hath Capri e'er supplied
Shelter to suffering worth? Have the divine
   Outpourings of high spirits sanctified
Its name and nature? Have the glorious Nine
   Left their memorial here? Or Sappho sighed—
Or Maro thundered? No! its soil is cursed
With memory of the bloated guilt it nursed!

CII.

Here throned, TIBERIUS battened on tne spoils   64
   Of lust and rapine: here, with rancorous hate
And vengeance—blasting as the flood that boils
   Beneath its caverns—held the thread of fate,
And smiled to hurl his victims 'mid the toils
   Of studied torture!—blood his game of state
Assassins for his guests—and fiends on watch
With murder's zest to heighten the debauch!

CIII.

But Mercy hath avenged her wrongs, and Peace

 Rebuilt her shrine. Here—if thou lovest a clime

Where health may flourish—rankling care decrease—

 And beauteous Nature smooth thy stream of time—

Here, in Campania's *Aprosapolis*,   65

 Repose! and feast thy soul with scene sublime—

Here, in thy concentrating gaze, condense

All earth's delights—all heaven's magnificence!

CIV.

The sunbeam shall not smite thee, for the sea

 Tempers its fervor; winter's kindly ray

Shall never chill thee, for the myrtle-tree,

 Pomegranate, palm and citron, shade the bay

With fruit and foliage; Nature's face shall be

 Thy book and mirror; one long summer day

Thy life; and, when at last thou takest thy rest,

Unfolding Spring shall fold thee in her breast!

CV.

But ye who, having suffered, best can tell,—

    Say, if the mourner *here* hath sorrowed less ?

If hearts revived that long had bid farewell

    To health, and health's delights, if loveliness

Hath conjured back her bloom ? recalled the spell

    Of Beauty's heritage ? Ye answer, " Yes !

We asked the *clime* of Phœbus—not his Art—

Those scenes that, while they soothe, exalt the heart !"

CVI.

Nature ! how fondly have I worshipped thee !

    Thy haunted shades my childhood's first delight !

Still gathering joy from each new mystery

    That flashed in fascination on my sight !

Thy lights and shadows—forests—lakes and sea—

    Heaven's starry pavement—blending day and night—

Thy voice my watchword, from the choral hymn

Of vernal groves to the volcano's brim !

CVII.

Wondrous in working—in her wildest freaks,

    What mystic powers irradiate Nature's form!

Whether in thunder or in song she speaks—

    Smiling in sunshine, or arrayed in storm—

Whether in her deep breast new toil she seeks,

    To mould a world—or animate a worm!—

Through every change, I hear her welcome voice

That woos me to her breast and says—Rejoice!

    *   *   *

CVIII.

Dread Possidoné! landmark of the past—   66

    Sole guardian of a nation's ashes!   How

I shrink into myself, to feel at last

    My foot within thy circle! Where thy brow—

Wrinkled with half the world's round years—hath cast

    Its spell around me! Melancholy thou—

But throned in majesty—proclaimest a race

Whose glory raised thee for its dwelling place!

CIX.

Temple and tomb—a Balbeck on the chart

   Of old renown! Struck with mysterious awe

I pace thy pillared avenues, and start

   Half doubtful, if the atmosphere I draw

Be earth's, and these the triumphs of man's art!

   Art thou amenable to milder law

Than Nature's common doom? that thus thy form

For twice twelve centuries braves the bolt and storm!

CX.

Colossus of the waste! Proud combination

   Of strength and beauty! Pointing to the time

When they, who raised thee for their adoration,   67

   Arose to found their empire in thy clime!

Prospered and passed—but left thee, in thy station

   Firm balanced—for their monument sublime!

That doom which swept a nation from thy base,

Enhanced thy grandeur's melancholy grace!

CXI.

It left thee mutually of gods and men

   The immortal chronicle! by these achieved—

To those devoted—in an era when

   Men emulated gods—like *theirs* believed

Their own brief sway eternal!   Now the fen

   And bulrush forest hide the soil that heaved

With their proud cities!   Such the ephemeral frame

Of mortal tenure, where man builds his fame!

CXII.

How are the mighty fallen!   A lifeless waste   68

   Limits the horizon!   And, where fields were fertile,

And fragrant harvests waved—and beauty graced

   Thy plain crowned with the Pæstan rose and myrtle!—

Broods noisome pestilence, and sullen-paced

   Browse the wild buffaloes!   In motley kirtle

The sibyl haunts my steps; and, gazing back,

The hovering bandit pounces on my track!   69

* * *

CXIII.

Sorrento ! while the hot sirocco blows   70

    And breathes exhaustion o'er each limb and look ;

Here, in thy citron groves, let me repose

    And lay me panting by the murmuring brook !

Here, while abroad the summer solstice glows,

    Be thou my nurse—lapt in some flowery nook

With vista to the bay !—no sweeter scene

Twixt Hadria's billows and thy blue Tyrrhene !

CXIV.

And lo, Night's shadows span the bay ! while beaming

    With all its mirrored stars, the tranquil blue

Of ocean slumbers : field and flower are teeming

    With summer's balm, and bright with falling dew.

Sweet voices are abroad : the air is gleaming

    With winged and fiery spangles—strange to view !

From every leaf electric sparks are glancing,   71

Where swift the firefly's twinkling troop are dancing.

CXV.

And, faithful to the hour, as stars that muster

   In nightly phalanx round heaven's shining camp—

Beneath yon palm—bright with unborrowed lustre

   The glow-worm kindles her connubial lamp—   72

Love's mimic cynosure !   What feelings cluster

   Within thy magic atmosphere, and stamp

Thy being with the joys, and fears, of earth !

Thy torch the symbol of domestic hearth !

CXVI.

Like thine, the watch-light of devoted love

   Brightens with darkness—holiest where retired !

Of peace enamoured, thus the mated dove

   Contrives her nest, by gentle love inspired :

Thus souls congenial taste delights above

   Earth's boasted bliss : and thus, my heart's admired !

Be thine the glow-worm's lamp—the dove's retreat—

And mine to whisper—Solitude is sweet !

CXVII.

But from the wanderer distant far art thou !

   Yet these I waft thee on Affection's wing !

While I must linger—as I linger now—

   Longing for those bright looks that wont to bring

More joy to me, than to the winter bough

   The leaves, and blossomed livery of Spring !

For here, though paradise surrounds my grot—

'Tis still a wilderness, where thou art not !

CXVIII.

But here I pause ; my lyre is cast aside ;

   To tell, with hopes deferred, the languid hour !

Little it recks, though colder hearts may chide

   The lay that soothes me in Sorrento's bower.   73

If still with me thy love and smile abide,!

   These are my fame !—thy pilgrim's richest dower !

But these denied—though heaven inspired his reed

And thousands praised—the bard were poor indeed !

CXIX.

And wilt thou prize what speaks to thee of him

   Whose love for thee o'er every ill prevailing

Still gathers fervour, as his day grows dim,

   And strengthens, as the strength of life is failing?

And wilt thou pray life's guardian seraphim

   To chase the blight his summer morn assailing?

Yes!—moved by *thee*, its balm shall heaven bestow,

And lengthen what thy love hath sweetened so!

     *   *   *

CXX.

Remnant of that bright sphere our fathers lost—

   Our being's sunshine—intellectual Mind!

Man's solace, and yet sorrow—bane, yet boast!

   Giving him wings to soar above his kind—

Hope in his hopelessness—comfort when crossed

   In worldly prospect! Yet, where most refined—

Most quickened to perceptions exquisite—

How far the pains o'erbalance the delight!

CXXI.

Albeit, 'tis sweet to feel the soul expanding—

 Through doubts and darkness, clearly to discern

Truths loved and longed for! and with grasp commanding

 The mines of science—learn, all man may learn,

Of earth and heaven—that all how little!   Standing

 On Fame's ambitious height, is but to yearn

For that which is beyond—some fatuous star

Still lures—and still misleads—thee from afar!

CXXII.

While living, chilled : half deified, when gone :

 Through life uncheered—neglected, and denied

Man's common courtesy !—how has the tone

 Of harps, heaven-strung, in bitter murmurs died !

But dead—mock gratitude decrees a *stone*

 To mark the spot the minstrel sanctified !

Upbraiding his cold ashes with a fame

That hath outlived all longing for a name !

CXXIII.

Man's feelings, like his features, are a part

  Of his peculiar frame : each hath its springs

That lock or loose the fountains of the heart—

  Each power to check or give the spirit wings—

And all their limits ! Wedded to his art,

  And vainly rash, the bard may sweep the strings—

But, save where heaven the votive chord hath fanned,

What discord wakes to his adventurous hand !

CXXIV.

That which hath cost him days—perchance of pain,

  And wakeful nights—nay, waste of life—shall seem,

To the cold world, born of a morbid brain—

  A thriftless song ! Yet, blameless if his theme,

The suffrage meant to sink, may save the strain !

  The world's opinion, like the Nubian stream,   74

Flows party-channelled,—but to him who knows

To persevere—at length united flows !

CXXVI.

Amid the world's crossways, the bristling thorns

    That wound the gentle—stimulate the bold :

Frowns that would freeze warm hearts the intrepid scorns—

    Content, by arduous struggle, as of old,

To *earn* his fame.   The light of life, like morn's,

    With various power impregnates the dull mould :

And blasts, which give the forest firmer root,

Will strip the vine, and blight the tropic's fruit.

CXXVII.

Art thou of Phœbus ?   Shrink not from the proof !

    Glows thy young heart with inspiration's fire ?

Improve the gift !   Stand firm—but stand aloof

    From all that would degrade the glorious lyre !

So minister in Virtue's high behoof!

    Through Nature's mystic workings still aspire

To Nature's Source !—Thus shalt thou subtilize

Thy song and, rising, teach man's soul to rise !

*　*　*

CXXVIII.

But *thou*, HYGËIA, whom the most I seek—
   Thou, of the rosy lip and sunny brow !
Hast thou no gift to glad my cheerless cheek,
   But dost forsake me like a sapless bough ?
Where shall I next thy partial smile bespeak ?—
   Where, to my fainting step and fruitless vow,
Wilt thou be found—a more propitious power—
In isles of Hellas, or Sicilian bower?

CXXIX.

, Twined with this mortal woof, Care mounts the car—
   The bark—the breeze ;—and, crossing Alps and sea,
Walks by my side ;—obscures the brightest star
   With ominous spots ;—from Pleasure's vernal tree
Shakes off the blossom !   Yet, sweet hours there are
   When—like a captive bird, the heart set free—
And nature, poured like music on the mind—
Sorrow, so long my comrade, lags behind !—

CXXX.

Choose as thou wilt; or wealth or fame pursue—
   Gird on the glaive—fly with the winged mast!
The phantom mocks, yet fascinates, thy view!—
   Lookest thou for sunshine?   Lo, the startling blast
Bursts o'er thy head!   That peace thy fancy drew
   Lives not on earth: the future, like the past,
Will still present its portion of alloy—
And furnish sorrow where it promised joy!

CXXXI.

'Tis well—I murmur not—nor to repine
   Hath my creed schooled me.   How should I forget
The health, and hope, and joy that *have* been mine!
   Earth's sweetest bonds dissolve—there is a debt
All flesh must pay!   Ere perfect day can shine,
   Life, like the natural sun, must wane and set—
Waiting the dawn!   The youngest, fairest shoot
Blooms but in death—the axe is at the root!

CXXXII.

'Tis well for man his destinies decree

   A day of ransom ! What a toil were life

If his ambition only were—To be !

   And be, by turns, the butt or tool of strife—

The dupe of hollow hearts, whose perfidy

   Strikes deadlier pang than the assassin's knife—

Beware !—and, seasoning candour with distrust,

Learn worldly lore, and to thyself be just !

CXXXIII.

Life's brevity is Nature's kindest boon :

   Made mortal, that immortal life may come—

So thou dost well, what boots it thee how soon

   Fate's welcome summons calls the wanderer home ?

Yet, dost thou sigh o'er youth's beclouded noon ?

   Alas, woes wait on all who farther roam !

Fresh tempests brood, and heaven's blue face deform,

But he who soundly sleeps, escapes the storm !

CXXXIV.

Life's first—youth's dearest—ties, where are ye? Gone

    The last dark voyage—never to return!

But where I follow.—Ye have left me lone

    To mourn, yet envy, your untimely urn!

But 'mid yon planetary worlds is one

    Where death-divided hearts, rekindled, burn!

This—this is balm! the hope we there shall meet

Souls that life's bitter draught made doubly sweet!

CXXXV.

I would not rob my soul of that fond thought,

    For all the realms that crowned the conquering Mede!

Rashly and vain 'gainst reason have they wrought,

    Who sap—self-blinded casuists—Nature's creed!

The first, firm truth by heaven's own spirit taught,

    And life's best balm—when balm it most doth need!

The pilgrim's pharos through a stormy world—

His buckler when the bolt of Death is hurled! . . . . .

CXXXVI.

Enough, 'tis midnight—night without a cloud !

   Salerno's promontory—isle and creek—

And Somma, by the lava-torrent ploughed—

   Baiæ, and Procida's volcanic peak

Seem strewn with pearls ! and with a voice endowed

   That scares repose :—in other tongues they speak—

'Tis meet that I should pause who long to earn

Of Nature's lore—and have so much to learn !

END OF CANTO SECOND.

HYMN TO THE VIRGIN.

LINES TO A SICILIAN AIR.

CHARYBDIS.

HYMN TO THE VIRGIN.

SALERNESE AIR.

———

Vo solcando un mar crudele
Senza vele,
E senza sarte :
Freme l'onda, il ciel s'imbruna,
Cresce il vento, e manca l'arte.—METAST.

Ave, MARIA ! glory's Queen !
 Our loadstar and defender—
Homage to thee, on shore and sea
 Our grateful spirits render !—
To thee—who guidest the fisher's bark,
 And lead'st the wildered stranger,
When all behind is drear and dark,
 And all before is danger :—
CHORUS—With fervent vow to thee we bow,
 The Friend that never faileth !
 When storms appear thou still art near
 To succour him that saileth !

Our wives are watching on the shore;
  Our children call their fathers ;
They quake to hear the tempest roar
  And tremble as it gathers !
The leven flashes on our bows—
  Yon mountain, rent asunder,
Writhes like a giant in his throes,
  And weeps in molten thunder !
CHORUS.—To thee, to thee we bow the knee,
      Our Friend that never faileth—
      In stormy sky thou still art nigh,
      To succour him that saileth !

No lingering star illumes our path,
  The night scowls drear and drearer !
But smiling through the tempest's wrath
  We know that Thou art nearer !
We know our wives and children keep
  Their fast before thine Altar :—
Thou wilt not leave their eyes to weep,
  Their faithful hearts to falter !
CHORUS.—To thee—to thee they bow the knee !
      Their Friend who never faileth,
      When tempests sweep the yawning deep
      To succour him that saileth.

Ave, MARIA! glorious Star!

    Where midnight horrors muster—

Thou givest the moon her silver car,

    The sky its holy lustre!

At thy behest the billows roar,

    At thy command they slumber!

Oh, softly guide our helm ashore,

    Whom night and storm encumber!

CHORUS.—With fervent vow to thee we bow—

        The Friend that never faileth,

        When tempests sweep the foaming deep,

        To succour him that saileth!

LINES,

TO A SICILIAN AIR.

Round my Rosalie's bower,
   To pleasure my fairest—
I'll plant every flower
   That is sweetest and rarest:
To wreathe thy bright hair
   Fresh garlands I'll bring thee—
And the nightingale there
   To slumber shall sing thee!

From the first ray of morn,
   When the day-star is waking;
Till the moon's silver horn
   Over Hybla is breaking—
And the birds from the boughs
   Wake their melodies o'er me—
Thy name's in my vows—
   Thy sweet image before me!

Then as onward I roam
   Through the deep forest darkling—
Sweet—sweet is my home
   With its lattice-light sparkling!
And bright stars above—
   But the star that is clearest
Is the signet of love—
   The dark eye of my dearest!

CHARYBDIS.

.

Dextrum Scylla latus, lævum implacata Charybdis . . . .
Tres Notus abreptas in saxa latentia torquet . . . .
. . . . ast illam ter fluctus ibidem
Torquet agens circum, et rapidus vorat æquore vortex.

'Tis the vesper hour—the leaf and flower

   Are strewn with sparkling pearls:

Ye hear but the groan from Ætna's cone—

Or the Zephyr's wing in the bowers of spring,

   And the wave where it crisps and whirls !

2

Round the crater's rim, clouds flash and skim;

   But hark, in Ste. Mergylla

The hymn is hushed—the crowd has rushed

From the sanctuary·---for " See, oh ! see—

   A ship's in the jaws of Scylla !"

3

A reckless bark, 'twixt light and dark,

　　O'er the rapid wave is bounding!

No oar is wet, no sail is set,

Yet her speed outstrips the strong-winged ships

　　In the channel that knows no sounding !

4

Hark ! from her deck, loud voices break

　　Mixed rage, despair, and rancour !

For now they discern, from stem to stern,

Their headlong course, and with frantic force

　　Unship the plunging anchor!

5

The capstan glows—down, down it goes—

　　Where anchor ne'er found pillow !

Yet Hope half streaks their bloodless cheeks—

'Tis brief—'tis vain !　The strong bower-chain

　　Has snapt like a sapless willow!

6

"On—on she goes, with her dashing bows—
  God help thee in thy danger!
None here—none here—can stay thy career!
Yon eddies boil to gorge their spoil—
  God help thee! reckless stranger!"

7

The boats unslung—to their oars they sprung—
  One faint last hope to rally;
But no more—no more—shall they weather the shore!
For the boat they urge—to the yawning surge
  Flies swifter than the galley!

8

Their strength has shrunk—their bold hearts sunk!
  A dismal doom hangs o'er them!
They fly in a track where no ship can tack!—
Above and below, are the shrieks of *woe!*
  And a fathomless gulf before them!

9

To the earth—to the sky—in their agony,

   Their farewell looks they lifted !

But here despair—destruction there—

Thro' the deepening gloom with the voice of doom—

   Pursued them as they drifted !

10

There, in foamy whirls Charybdis curls—

   Loud Scylla roars to larboard !

In that howling gulf, with the dog and wolf,*

Deep moored to night, with her living freight,

   That goodly ship is harboured !

---

* See *Mythology*. Ovid and other poets have painted Scylla with *dogs* only; but Virgil has heightened the portrait by the addition of *wolves*.

    Feris atram *canibus* succingitur alvum, &c.—Ov. Met. lib. xiii.
    .... Delphinum caudas utero commissa *luporum.*—Virg. Æn. iii.

The ebb and flood in this Strait are very irregular and strong ; and, where it is narrowest, extremely impetuous, so that there is no stemming the tides when the wind blows strong from the *southward*. At this period ships are often caught in the eddies—whirled about with the greatest rapidity, and not unfrequently lost. Under other circumstances the Strait is so smooth that the smallest boat may navigate it with safety.

NOTES TO CANTO II.

1.

. . . . Sage laws—paternal sway.

These are expressly applicable to Tuscany in the present day; nowhere are the affairs of government conducted with greater mildness. The happiness and prosperity of the people are become proverbial—their country is the " political *oasis* of Italy."

3.

And baffled Turnus battles for his bride!

> Vicisti: et victum tendere palmas
> Ausonii videre: tua est *Lavinia* conjux.

4-5.

Exclaim with patriot pride—These—these are ours!

Such is the language of the modern Roman, whenever the conversation turns upon the ancient glory of his country, contrasted with its present divisions, jealousies, and church despotism. *Son Romano io !* So often retorted upon the suspicious traveller, seems almost a burlesque upon that once proud title—but it is a spark which shews that the fire, though stifled, is not quite extinct.—*Gl' Italiani comminciano anch' essi a pensare !*

6.

Syrtis—Charybdis.

> Perque procellosas *Syrtes*, per saxa Maleæ . .
> Tumidis torta Charybdis, &c.

G

7.

" *Concord.*"—The temple of CONCORD in Rome is still one of her most imposing relics.

8.

Distant yet not dim
The eternal city glimmers from her hills.

To an eye accustomed to contemplate prospects through a vaporous sky, nothing can be more pleasing than the extreme purity of the atmosphere, and the distinct appearance of remote objects in this climate.

9.

Causeways that drain the distant hills in Rome.

These aqueducts are, beyond all others, the most stupendous monuments of Roman architecture—such as at first sight fix the attention, and excite the astonishment, of every traveller. The aqueduct which forms the allusion in the text, is that seen to greatest advantage from the Esplanade of the Lateran, about sunset.

10.

No Tully fulmines in her forum now.

" Fulmined over Greece."—" Eloquii fulmen."

11.

Procida.

Prochyta of the ancients. (The modern pronunciation of this— Protch-ida—with a host of others, seem to start a fresh subject for philologists on the *chi*, Latin—*ci*, Italian—and χ, Greek).

With regard to the natural beauties of this island, no Roman of the present day at least, but willingly subscribes to the predilection of Juvenal. *Vel ego Prochytam præpono Saburræ!*

Ischia. The ancient *Inarime.* Typhæus's prison; but the fire of whose eyes, like the volcano, has been long extinct. Berkely, Bishop of Cloyne, often declared that the happiest summer he ever enjoyed was in this island, which he called an epitome of the earth.

Nisita. In front of this fairy islet the pilgrim performs quarantine —anciently *Nesis.* See Lucan, vɪ.—90. *Emittit, &c.*

12.

Syren of the sea.

Vide Vɪʀɢ. Geoʀɢ. ɪv. v. 564. Homeʀ Oᴅ. 12. Sᴛʀᴀʙ. ɪ—v.

13.

Tasso's *Muse.*

His birth-place; the scene of his happiest hours. See his Life, by Roscoe.

14.

Look but on Naples, say her bards, and die.

The view from the Gulf of Naples is unrivalled—even by that on the Bosphorus. It has one decided advantage over Byzantium, in the extraordinary character of its mountains, among which, *Vesuvius* is a feature of intense interest. The pilgrim who rides his first quarantine off Naples, enjoys a fascinating panorama of those ancient localities which take such powerful hold of the imagination. The *proverbs* alluded to are well known: " *Un pezzo di cielo caduto in terra!*" " *Vede Napoli e mori!*"

15.

This electric soil.

This is abundantly evident both in the natural and moral soil. See a book of travels.

16.

. . . . And simmering the broad bay
Heaves o'er a forge.

The basin or gulf is supposed to have been, and is still called, the *crater.*

G 2

For illustration of the text, see—or read the history of *Nero's Baths*—wood near the *Avernus* and *Solfatara*.   In the latter, a stick thrust into the soil, or rather crust, where I stood, caught fire; and, for the benefit of my shoemaker, and a rather unseasonable gratification of curiosity, I made similar observations, though more sensibly felt, in an ascent of Vesuvius.   Ladies would do well in similar enterprises to line their *chaussure* with *asbestos.*

17.

Here, in their beds of lava, cities sleep!

Namely, Herculaneum, Pompeii, Stabia, &c.

18.

Capuchins—preaching friars, &c.

19.

Illuminated folio, &c.

As objection may be taken to this homely simile, I must state—if in apology—that I yet know of nothing that to my own mind conveys so correct an idea of the brilliancy of colouring and the rich variety which emblazon and *peculiarize* the evening picture here attempted.   It was the *first* idea that struck the writer as a *spectator.*

20.

The Improvisatore, &c.

This imposing personage, as some may regret to hear, is much less frequent, though not less attractive, than in former years.   This peripatatic poet, wit, and commentator on Tasso, has lost half his audience on the Môle; the preaching friar is in a still worse predicament; and even Pulcinello has experienced a defalcation in his revenue.*

* "Change of Air," by Dr. Johnson.

21.

Where their sepulchres rise by the sea.

For an account of these tombs see *Memoria di un antico Sepol-creto Greco-Romano, da Lorenzo Giustiniani.*

22.

Sweet Posilippo!

(Magni tumulis adcanto *magistri!*) apparently ἀπο της πυυσεως της λυπης—or " Sorrow's rest," as the etymon would import. A title conferred upon it by its primitive colonists, who, having made trial of its soil and climate, laid down their burdens and took up their abodes on its shore.

23.

Who sleeps below?

Mantua me genuit : Calabri rapuere : tenet nunc
Parthenope.   Cecini Pascua, Rura, Duces.

Tunc sacrum felix aluisti, Terra, Maronem
    Tunc pio celas ossa beato sinu ?
Anne etiam, ut fama est, Vatis placidissima sæpe
    Inter odoratum cernitur umbra nemus ?

24.

. . . . . *Here Boccacio for the Lyre*
Renounced the world!

See his life.—*Lives of the Italian Poets.*

25.

. . . . *She whose bier*
Was the unbowelled mountain.

Pompëia! (Pompeii, or Pompeia.) This subject has become so familiarized to every class of readers, that it would be superfluous, if not presumptuous, to extend my notes beyond the immediate allusions in the text. I may add, however, that my observations were made on the spot, which I have attempted—however inadequately—to describe; and further, that I know of no other scene, or *spectacle*, that takes such immediate and entire hold of the mind and imagination; and which no change, nor circumstance, of afterlife can ever obliterate. Let him, who travels for excitement, visit Pompeii by moonlight, and view an eruption of Vesuvius from the bay at midnight!

26.

Sarno's tortured tide, &c.

The sympathy here alluded to has been uniform and remarkable in all eruptions. See particularly those of 1631 and 1698; also *Parrini* and *Boccone*, who adduce some remarkable facts on this subject.

27.

Upwards of twenty human skeletons were found in the cellar of a house near the gate, and opposite that (an *inn*) marked with the *Salve* of welcome, seven skeletons: the first carried a *lamp*, and of the others, each retained betwixt its bony fingers something which it had wished to preserve.

28.

In 1812, among other exhumations, a skeleton was found near the Tragic Theatre, with a purse in its grasp containing, I am informed, eight pieces of gold, three hundred and sixty of silver, and forty-two of bronze; the purse of cloth, and still maintaining its precious deposit in due form!

29.

Their city a vast sepulchre, their hearth
A charnel house.

Dio informs us, lib. lxvi., that the inhabitants were surprised by the eruption, while the circus was crowded with spectators. This is disputed ; but I perfectly agree with Dr. James Johnson, that the skeletons already discovered constitute a very small proportion of those who actually perished. Little more than *an eighth* part of the city is yet excavated ! How much, therefore, remains to unriddle the mystery that hangs over its last awful struggles ! *

30.

The marks of wine-cups are still visible on the marble counter.

31.

There is no exaggeration in the text—there lie the materials half finished, and in various stages of their progress, as they were originally placed for his operations, and as they were left by the last workman, 1700 years ago.

32.

Isis' shrine.

As described in the text. Close to the cella of this temple, a skeleton was discovered. The sacred vessels, lamps and tables, though removed, are still shown at the *Museo.*

33.

Hollowed by the rolling car.

The tracks of the wheels which anciently rolled over the pavement, have a powerful effect in conjuring back the *past*—the busy multitude that once thronged the now silent thoroughfare.

34.

. . *Door, writ with the name of its last tenant.*

This I remarked in several instances. The scribblings and drawings of the soldiers on the walls of their barracks are quite distinct.

---

* By a letter just received from Pompeii, (Feb.) I am gratified to learn that the excavations are proceeding, though at intervals, with more than ordinary decision.

35.

EUMACHIA.

I have met with nothing in sculpture more beautiful than this: there is a fascination in the features and expression, heightened no doubt by the circumstances of the place, which to my fancy surpasses even the presiding divinity in the *Tribunal* at Florence; but this opinion is no *authority*. The arrangement of the drapery displays exquisite taste and execution.

36-7.

Street of Sepulchres.

Beyond the gate. The tomb of the priestess Mammia is remarkable. Here are still preserved undisturbed the ancient family urns and ashes, on small altars within the monuments; externally are the broken masks.

38.

If 'twixt the seething lava and the shower, &c.

Pompeia, as the reader well knows, was buried by showers of *ashes*—Herculaneum overwhelmed by torrents of boiling *lava*. The former comparatively, offers but little obstruction to the labourer; but the latter, having insinuated itself in the consistence of molten lead, into every crevice, and become indurated like marble, requires the skill and perseverance of a miner to dislodge it, and that by very slow degrees.

39.

Some cursing called their gods.

See Pliny's description of Pompeia's last day.—Many called on the gods for assistance, others despaired of the existence of the gods, &c.

40-1.

The lofty circus vault and corridor.

This theatre was one of the most perfect specimens of ancient architecture. It was capable of containing from three thousand to four thousand spectators :—nearly the whole of its surface—as well as the arched corridor leading to the seats, was cased with marble, and the area floored with massive squares of precious *giallo-antico.*

41.

And last he led me to a bust, whereon, &c.

Upon whatever plausible grounds the antiquarian, or other learned annotator, may *dispute* this point, they can adduce no *proof* to overthrow the popular belief. There is nothing in the whole collection which makes so forcible an appeal to the heart and the imagination as *this.*

42.

What city hath returned to earth again?

In this respect these cities stand awful and solitary monuments. The finest pulpits in the world for homilies on the instability of human glory!

43.

" Like a child gathering pebbles on the shore."—*Sir Isaac Newton.*

44.

Baiæ.

> Varia circum oblectamina vitæ
> . . . blandissima littora, Baias.—*Stat.*

> Littus beatæ aureum veneris !
> Baiæ superbæ blanda dona naturæ.—*Mart.*

Cimmerian Cumæ.

> Ενδα δε Κιμμερεων ανδρων δημός τε πόλις τε
> 'Ηέρι καὶ νεφέλη κεκαλυμμέναι οὐδέ ποτ'αὐτοὺς
> 'Ηέλιος φαέθων ἐπιδέρκεται ακτινεσσιν, &c. &c.

Acheron.—See ancient classics.

Avernus.—" Stagna inter celebrem nunc mitia." Such is its character at the present moment.

ELYSIAN FIELDS.

> Devenere locos lætos et amœna vireta
> Fortunatorum nemorum, sedesque beatas.

Sibyl's Grotto.—At the time I penetrated the recesses of this labyrinth, the bottom was covered to a considerable depth with stagnant water: and though mounted on the shoulders of a sturdy lazzaroni, still it is not an experiment to be recommended—to invalids at least.

PLINY.

> . . . Ubi dies redditus, corpus inventum est integrum . . .
> Habitus corporis quiescenti, quam defuncto similior.

45.

LUCULLUS.

For particulars *vide* Plutarch, in Lucull. This prince of choice spirits had other villas of equal, but various, magnificence—changing his residence with the storks and cranes. He purchased the villa of Marius alone for a sum equal to eighty thousand pounds sterling. His *Villa Misenensis* (transformed into a monastery A. D. 488) was unrivalled for its site and artificial embellishments.

> . . . Monte summo posita Luculli manu,
> *Prospectat* Siculum et *prospicit* Tuscum mare.

46.

Sybaris. Vide history of that luxurious city.

47-8.

NERO.　　　.　.　.　*Parricide and charioteer.*

For illustration of the latter *vide* Tacit. Annal. lib. xiv. s. 14. For that of the former *vide* ibid., sect. 4—10.

50.

LINTERNUM.

Torre di Patria. Here Scipio Africanus retired to voluntary exile. The *torre* is the only vestige of the city as well as of Scipio—the epitaph is universally known.

INGRATA PATRIA, NE QUIDEM OSSA MEA HABES.

See the eloquent declamation of Seneca (Epist. lxxxvi.) also Liv.
lib. xxxviii. 53.

51.

CICERO.

"Romani fama decusque fori." "Eloquii fulmen." See his orations
passim. Here in his villa of *Puteolanum* Cicero composed his Aca-
demic Questions.

52.

Puteoli.

Pozzuoli.—See Senec. Nat. Quæst. lib. iii. c. 20. Plin. lib. xxxv. c. 13.
Quis enim satis miretur *pessimam* ejus (terræ) partem ideoque *pulverem*
appellatum in Puteolanis, *collibus opponi maris fluctibus mersumque
protinus fieri lapidem inexpugnabilem undis, et fortiorem quotidie.*

Here the *Via Appia* terminates, and exhibits, in various points, its
ancient indestructibility.

On the beach I gathered various fragments of precious mosaic,
thrown up by the sea. The *Duomo* (anciently the temple of Antinous!)
and temple of Jupiter Serapis, are the objects alluded to in the text.

53.

Mightiest of the Twelve.

See Acts Apostles, c. xxviii.

54.

Tramontana.

See Note 2—27, Canto First.

55.

. . . . *Man's purest creed,*
Christian as Epictetic.

Vide Summary of Epictetus's creed. Ανέχυ και άπέχυ.

56.

A volcano, says Eustace, is the most tremendous phenomenon presented to the eyes of mortals. All the agitation of earthquakes—all

the crash of thunders—all the horrors of darkness—all the blaze of lightnings—and all the rage of conflagration—are united and armed with tenfold terror in an *eruption*. Its appearance and effects seem not to announce the arm of the Almighty extended to chastise and correct at the same time; but resemble the rage of *demons* broke loose from their prison, *armed with the flames of hell* to disfigure nature and to ravage the creation. (See also Plin. jun. lib. vi. Epist. 20.) Every thing contributes to fill the mind with the most awful *satisfaction*. Beyond doubt one of the most grand and terrific which nature presents, and affords an *enjoyment* which I have no power to describe.—*Horsfield*.

57.

The eruptions of *Vesuvius* are more striking than those of Ætna, in as much as the former are more within the scope of observation—and rarely burst but with the probability of destruction to human life and habitations. Vesuvius, A. D. 473, covered, according to Marcell. Comes, all Europe with its ashes. " Nocturnisque in die tenebris: omnem Europam faciem minuto contegit pulvere." But on this subject see any book of travels—more particularly Sir W. Hamilton's account.

As the best position for a silent contemplation of the scene (when such a scene presents itself!) I would recommend that off the *Castel del' Uovo* —and about a mile out on the bay. But if the modern *Pliny* be withal an invalid, let him act accordingly and by advice—it is a scene that will amply repay him for every inconvenience but dangerous illness.

Furies, &c.—See Dion Cassius, lib. xvi.

58.

Dread Sympathy.   Stanza xc.

The subterraneous communications, and simultaneous agitation of these Phlegræan storehouses, are not the least remarkable part of their history—the sympathy between Vesuvius and *Solfatara* is strikingly so.

59.

Vesper Hymn.

See the hymn appended to this canto.

60.

Tarantella—the national dance.

Thunderer's Forge, by an inscription at Capua (*vide* Parini) Vesuvius appears to have been consecrated to *Jupiter Tonans,* viz., JOVI . VESUVIO . SACRUM, D. D.

61.

Returning Revels.—This was never more remarkable than in the great eruption of 1707; when the people flocking out of the town to see the fiery torrent from the mountain, and observing that *it began to harden,* abandoned themselves to the grossest *lupercalia.*

The generality here, says an old traveller, are like *sailors,* who never think of heaven or hell but in imminent danger; and, as soon as that is over, return to their former wicked practices.

St. Gennaro, it is well known, has a patent for locking up or arresting the lava at any given point. (See the *inscription* to this saint.) It is quite evident that their critical locality on the immediate confines of two worlds—brimstone and boiling lava ! causes no disquietude to these happy people. "Dum vivimus, *vivamus !*" is the watchword. But one step, truly, from the most awfully sublime to the contemptibly ridiculous—from the doomsday thunders of an *eruption* to the festive squeaks of *Pulcinello.*

62.

Dead but a few brief hours.—It is lamentable that so many cases of premature interment should be daily hazarded in obedience to the law on this subject. I need hardly add that the stranger who made himself available in the present instance, was not an *Asclepiades.* Over-hasty interments, as we learn from *Pliny,* Hist. Nat. l. xxvi. c. 3, were not uncommon among the ancients. Was it not the deplorable misfortune of *Duns Scotus ?* Who has not heard of the Norman lord *Louis de Cirille—the thrice buried ?* It is matter of concern that real narratives of this kind should be obscured and brought into disrepute by other absurd fictions. Visiting, a few days since, the church of *S. Giovanni Pappacodi,* I learnt that the founder Pappacodi was buried in a fit, and came to life again. A relation, on advice of his death, coming post to town, three days after the funeral, ordered the disinterment, and found that the deceased had bruised himself by struggling, and entirely altered his posture.

63.

Conrad.

See the history of the time, 1269.—CHARLES deshonora sa victoire par les cruautés qu'il exerça sur les vaincus . . . . la plus memorable victime qu'il immola à sa vengeance, fut l'infortuné CONRADIN— dernier rejéton de la maison de *Souabe* . . il monta sur l'échafaud . . les seuls mots qu'il prononça furent ceux-ci;

> *O ma pauvre mère! quelle douleur sera la tienne!*

On pretend que la terre imbibée de son sang, en conserve les traces . . . . qu'on y remarque un endroit humide, qui est comme une tâche, qu'on ne voit ailleurs. . . . *Hist. Repub. Ital.*

64.

TIBERIUS.

> *Quem rupes Caprearum tetra latebit*
> *Incesto possessa Seni?*—CLAUD. DE IV. Cons. Hor.

See Tacit. Annal. lib. xii.—xx. He may be truly said to have realized Βιος κυκλώπειος—quæ neque legibus, neque disciplina civili constet, neque religione deorum gubernetur.

65.

Aprosapolis.—The name given by AUGUSTUS, as characteristic of this delicious spot. " La douceur de l'air qui règne dans toute la Campagne Felice, se fait encore plus sentir ici—*c'est la patrie des Zéphyrs!* J'ai ambitionné (says the Abbé Coyer) le sort d'un voyageur Anglais qui enchanté du local, et du climat, a fini les tous ses voyages en établissant dans une jolie maison." There is not, however, at present, I understand, any English traveller so agreeably lodged. I need not add that the description in the text falls far short of the locality.

66-9.

Possidoné.

Pæsidonia, Paestum.—For nine centuries these ruins, though probably not *unknown*, were unnoticed by any traveller, and were only announced to the world about the middle of last century, as a most interesting discovery, and recognised as the last gigantic remains of *Possidone.* With respect to the founders we possess no authentic records—nothing beyond plausible conjecture. The mystery which hangs over them gives them an interest peculiarly their own ; while the monuments themselves leave an impression upon the mind never to be effaced.

If, according to Mazzochi, the city was founded by a colony of Dorians, these temples must have seen the full complement of years mentioned in the text, and with a little care would see as many more.

Pæstan rose.—Victura rosaria Pæsti—*biferi* rosaria Pæsti.

> Vidi Pæstano gaudere rosaria cultu
> Exoriente novo roscida Lucifero.

The reader will remember the tragical fate of an English gentleman and his lady in this immediate neighbourhood. Unless well escorted a visit to Pæsto is still a perilous enterprise.

70.

Sirocco. . . . . Madidis Notus evolat alis.—*Ov.*
. . . . Madidus *tepido* sibilat ore Notus.

> O quis me gelidis sub vallibus Hæmi
> Sistat.

For some excellent practical observations on the subject of these transitions, see Change of Air, by Dr. Johnson ; they are the latest, and—if I may express an opinion founded on personal experience, and some painful familiarity with the subject—the best I have met with.

The glow-worm kindles her connubial lamp.

(Cicindela) is the *wingless female* of a beetle insect. The light, which is of a beautiful sulphur colour, proceeds from the last three rings of the body. It is phosphorescent, and so strong that it will show itself through several folds of paper, and has the power of absorbing light, and of giving it out at pleasure.

From the circumstance of the male being a *winged* insect, and the female not, it was necessary that some contrivance should be had recourse to for directing the rambler to his sedentary mate. What more beautiful—and at the same time efficient—guide could possibly be contrived than this self-lighted hymeneal torch?

73

Sorrento. . . . A vertice Surrentino

Tyrrheni speculatrix virgo profundi.—*Stat. Syl.*

Vitabant æstus qua pinguia culta vadosus
Irrigat et placido cursu petit æquora Sarnus,
Grata quies nemorum, manantibus undique rivis,
Et Zephyris densas inter crepitantibus alnos.—*Sannazaro.*

Beneath palm-trees, or amid the evergreen groves of orange-trees, covered with odorous fruit and sweet-scented leaves, mere existence is a pleasure, and even the pains of disease are sometimes forgotten amidst the balmy influence of Nature.—*Sir H. Davy.*

Nubian Stream.—The two great streams from Abyssinia, *blue* and *white,* unite—as the reader well knows—in Nubia, and form the Nile.

74

Who knows to persevere.

Μελέτη το πᾶν. *Periand.*

END OF THE NOTES TO CANTO SECOND.

BOUND
1985.

CPSIA information can be obtained
at www.ICGtesting.com
Printed in the USA
BVOW04s1135181017
498002BV00010B/267/P